M000072847

Thank God You're Lazy!

The Instant Cure for What's Holding You Back

By Dr. Rob Gilbert
and Coach Mike Tully

1st Edition, Mike Tully
ISBN 978-1478366430 Published by TotalGamePlan, Inc.
900 Valley Road D-1, Clifton, NJ, 07013
Publishing date: Sept. 2012

DEDICATIONS

To my mother, Corinne Ellis Gilbert, on the occasion of her 90th birthday. My mother could never have written this book because she knows nothing about laziness. She doesn't have a lazy bone in her body. At one stage of her life she managed a household with four generations: her mother, her husband, her daughter and her grandson. Now at age 90, she is young, vibrant, curious and drives better than I do! How do you do it? Wow!

I also dedicate this book to my co-author, Coach Mike Tully. Mike had to depend on me for a lot of the first-hand information on what it's like to be lazy because he's a lot like my mom. He's a husband, father, grandfather, coach, editor, speaker, writer, friend and all-around great guy. All he knows about being lazy is second-hand information. Mike, thanks for teaching me how to be unlazy and coaching me to finish this book. – ROBERT ELLIS GILBERT

To my wife, Patty, who is never lazy, especially when helping others. To my co-author Dr. Rob Gilbert, a friend, mentor and an inspiration, not to mention the person who conceived this book. To Gary Pritchard, a motivator wherever he goes. To Patty Sullivan, who makes lives better every day. To Coach Scott Illiano, who leads with principle and purpose. – MIKE TULLY

Special thanks to editors Sue Brooks, Sarah Weiswasser and Larry O'Connor.

Cover image by Shutterstock.

TABLE OF CONTENTS

LETTER FROM THE AUTHORS

Dear Reader:

Here's what we don't know about you:
1. We don't know what you do.
2. We don't know how well you do it.

Here's what we do know about you:
1. Whatever level you're on, you want to get to the next one. You have that drive inside you that wants more.
2. The one thing that's keeping you from getting to the next level is laziness. You know what you have to do – you're just not doing it. It's that simple.

Here's what we want you to know about us:
1. We can help you defeat your laziness and get to that next level. As teachers and coaches, we've already helped thousands of people do this.
2. We don't want this to be another "thought-provoking" book. We wrote this book to be "change-provoking." This book is meant to change you from lazy to motivated!

Here are two steps you can take right now:
1. Start reading this book immediately. It's amazing how many people buy a book and never read it. Why? Because they're lazy!
2. Finish this book as soon as possible. It's amazing how many people start a book and never finish it. Why? Because they're lazy!

Here's the most important news:
1. The bad news: Nobody, including you, ever wants to be accused of being lazy. It hurts even if it's true.

2. The good news: Thank God you're lazy! Laziness can be
   cured instantly. And this instant cure for laziness is in
   your hands right now.

Let's get started,

Gilbert & Tully

CHAPTER ONE

THE DISEASE

"The generality of mankind is lazy. What distinguishes men of genuine achievement from the rest of us is not so much their intellectual powers and aptitudes as their curiosity, their energy, their fullest use of their potentialities."
— SYDNEY J. HARRIS

"The lazy fox catches no poultry."
— BENJAMIN FRANKLIN

"Today we fight. Tomorrow we fight. The day after, we fight. And if this disease plans on whipping us, it better bring a lunch, 'cause it's gonna have a long day doing it."
— JIM BEAVER

"Disease is the biggest money-maker in our economy." — JOHN H. TOBE

THE BIGGEST MISTAKE PEOPLE MAKE

Deep down inside, you want to be great. You may not want to admit it, but it's true. Want proof? Why would you be reading this if you didn't want more from your life?

You've fantasized about being a great athlete, a famous musician or the owner of your own company. You would enjoy the prestige, the satisfaction and, okay, the money.

Most of all, you would love the sense that you have finally done what you're capable of doing. But that can't happen yet because you're making a mistake. What would you think of a situation like this?

1. You're sick.
2. You go to the doctor.
3. Good news! The doctor knows exactly what's wrong.
4. The doctor gives you a prescription that will cure you.
5. You drive to the drugstore.
6. The druggist fills your prescription.
7. You go home.
8. End of story.

What's wrong with the story? You never took the medication. You didn't take action. You knew what to do but you didn't do it.

Sound ridiculous? Not really. We see it happen every day in some form or another. People buy gym memberships but never go. They get into college but don't study. They start a career but don't work at it.

They're all making the same mistake: They're letting laziness stop them. It's the biggest mistake people make.

THE LAZINESS DEMONSTRATION
(Dr. Gilbert speaking)

I have been a college professor for more than 33 years. A lot has changed over that time, but the format of my final exams never varies. First of all, I don't even call them exams. I call them Laziness Demonstrations.

Why???

Because I do everything I can to help my students get an A. At the beginning of each semester, I tell them what the exam format will be. Two weeks before the test, I give out the questions. We spend the last two weeks of the semester going over the answers. The day after the exam, students can e-mail me for their grades, and, if they don't like them, they can retake the exam as many times as they want until they get the grade they want.

Let's repeat that: They can retake the exam as many times as they want until they get the grade they want.

Right now you're probably thinking, "I wish I had a professor like that because everyone would get an A."

But everyone doesn't get an A. Some students even get an F. One semester, almost half the class failed the course!

Why?

Because they're lazy.

And that's why I give exams this way. To show the students that life itself is a laziness demonstration. If you aren't getting what you want in life, it's because you are lazy.

LAZINESS DEMONSTRATION IN ACTION
(Coach Tully speaking)

Could what Dr. Gilbert said about laziness actually be true? Could people really flunk a test in which they've been given the questions AND the answers? AND the chance to take it again?

Using Dr. Gilbert's example, I tried a Laziness Demonstration of my own.

My English students were young and very worried about their final exam, so I told them not to stress. "There will be only two questions on the test," I said, "and I will give you the answers to both of them."

One of the questions involved a quote in a play. In the days before the test, we went over who said the quote, and why the message was important. We did this several times.

When the test came, most of the pupils did well. But some did not. One or two could not even identify who said the quote!

That was after I told them what would be on the exam, and what the answer would be. Several times.

Those pupils failed, and it had nothing to do with their ability. I hope they won't be going through life saying they're "not good at Shakespeare." They failed because they were lazy.

DON'T TAKE OUR WORD FOR IT

If you don't believe us about people being lazy, this student, who actually took one of Dr. Gilbert's Laziness Demonstrations, will attest to where laziness can lead.

"I had Dr. Gilbert for my freshman seminar. He gave us the Laziness Demonstration for our final. After I took the test, I e-mailed him for my grade and I got a C. When he e-mailed me the grade, he also e-mailed when I could take the test again if I wanted to. I was so lazy that I never retook the test, and settled for a C in the class. Laziness got to me!"

At least she admits it. There's no deep, dark secret for this student. She doesn't have to pour out her heart on "Oprah" or get into a hair-pull on "Jerry Springer." She doesn't have to spend lots of money on a cure. There are no complicated reasons for why she got a C in a course in which she easily could have earned an A. Laziness got to her!

Don't believe us about being lazy. Believe someone who is living proof.

This student was lazy, but at least she admitted it. That's a start. If she wants to get the things that she wants, she has to find a way to become unlazy.

THE DIRTY LITTLE SECRET

You're lazy.

There, we said it. How do we know? Because everyone is lazy in some way or another. Did this ever happen to you? It happens to 48 percent of college students! You graduated from high school and were accepted to a college. You enrolled and did poorly. So you dropped out or you flunked out. If you were ever asked why you didn't graduate, you'd say something like, "I wasn't college material," or "I wasn't smart enough." Or you might even think to yourself that some teachers were unfair ...

None of that is true. The simple truth is: You were lazy!!! You didn't put in the time or the effort to study.

Want proof? No college would ever admit you if it didn't think you had what it takes to graduate.

No college wants people to fail out.

All colleges want and need alumni.

Your college wanted you to succeed. Your college had help for people doing poorly. Your college did everything it could. If you did terribly in school it was because you were lazy!

Maybe the example about college doesn't apply to you. Maybe you're lazy when it comes to staying in shape, or calling on clients, or practicing your free throws. Whatever it is, something is keeping you from greatness.

Remember, the only thing that keeps you from getting what you want is laziness.

THE COSTLIEST PARKING TICKET EVER
(Dr. Gilbert speaking)

Before you throw down this book in a frustrated rage, realize that we are not condemning you – we are coaching you. I wish someone had coached me a certain day in Passaic, NJ.

That's the day I got a parking ticket. If I had gone online, I could've paid it in less than five minutes – but I was too lazy to do that.

About a month later, I received a letter saying that since I missed my court date, the fee had been increased.

Of course, I could've gone online and paid the ticket – but I was too lazy to do that.

About a month later, I received a letter stating that my license had been suspended.

The next day, I drove – illegally – to the Passaic County courthouse and, after waiting about three hours, I paid a fee of about $150.00 (for a ticket that originally was $30.00).

When I gave the clerk my check, I said under my breath, "Thank God this nightmare is over."

She said, "It's not over yet. You've paid your fine, now you have to go to the Division of Motor Vehicles because your license is still suspended."

Another three hours and another couple hundred bucks later, I finally drove home – legally!

All that money and all that time – just because I was lazy.

If you're doing lousy in school – the culprit is laziness.

If you're not producing in sports – the culprit is laziness.

If you're doing poorly in business – the culprit is laziness.

But here's a secret before we move on. We were going to write this book five years ago. But we were lazy. See? It's not just you.

"You are 100 percent responsible for how you choose to respond to everything that happens in your life."
— UNKNOWN

RELEASE YOUR BRAKES

Suppose you get a new car and proudly take it out on the road. You notice right away that it doesn't seem to be moving the way you want it to. After a day or two of waiting to see if things work themselves out, you take the car to the mechanic.

Is it the engine? The transmission? What is it?

"Well," says the mechanic, "you were driving with the emergency brake on."

Our lives are like that car. We are machines designed for success, but we get in our own way. We look under the hood for excuses: We don't have the ability. We're too small. We're not smart enough.

Forget the fancy reasons. You're lazy! And laziness is nothing more than a reaction to the things that happen around you.

You don't have control over what happens to you. You don't have control over what happens around you. But you do have control over how you react to what happens to you. Remember this quote: "I am 100 percent responsible for how I choose to respond to everything that happens in my life."

If your life is not moving along like a finely tuned car, don't look for fancy excuses. Instead, ask yourself if you are giving full effort. Gandhi said, "Full effort is full victory."

You can start on your way to victory right now.

THE WORLD'S MOST MISSPELLED WORD

At this point you may be ready to punch us out. You say you had an unreasonable teacher or a coach who didn't like you or a boss who played favorites.

All of the above are called *rationalizations*. Here's something you should know about rationalizations. It's all in how you spell the word "rationalize."

For the purposes of this book, it's spelled:

RATIONAL LIES

When you rationalize, you're telling yourself "rational lies," like "I had an unreasonable teacher" or "My coach didn't like me," etc. ...

Rational lies.

What mistakes do students make on the Laziness Demonstration that keep them from getting an A? They aren't in class when the questions are given out. They miss some or all of the review classes. They fail to e-mail the day after the exam for their grade. And, believe it or not, they receive the questions, they show up for the review, they e-mail but they don't retake the exam when they get less than an A.

If they blame their bad grade on anything but the reasons above, they are telling themselves **rational lies**.

Remember the car with the emergency brake on? When people fail, they blame the machine. They don't blame the driver. Stop telling yourself rational lies.

THE TRUTH AND THE LIE

"Why aren't you doing better in school?" When we ask students this question, they say things like, "I'm just not smart enough," or "I can't learn foreign languages," or "I'm lousy at math."

Nothing could be further from the truth! Basically these students are claiming that they lack the mental hardware to get the job done. They're lying – and they don't even realize it.

THE LIE: You're not "intellectually blessed enough" to get great grades.

THE TRUTH: You're not getting great grades because you're lazy!

Success in school, sports, sales, etc., has nothing to do with INTELLIGENCE, and everything to do with DILIGENCE.

If you're not getting the grades you want, making the teams you want, or making the money you want – repeat after us, "I am lazy."

Now at least you're telling the truth.

When you say, "I am lazy," it means that you're not using your potential. When you say, "I'm not smart," it means that you think you don't have the potential. The good news is that you're lazy.

Laziness is a disease that you can easily cure.

UNLAZY HALL OF FAME
Oprah Winfrey

If you tried to create a blueprint for a life of trouble and sadness, it might go something like this:

* Extreme poverty

* Teenage runaway

* Unwanted pregnancy

* Taunted by peers

* Sexually abused

Far from resulting in a failed life, these circumstances merely became obstacles for Oprah Winfrey to overcome.

Using a gift of gab that her family observed from her earliest years, Winfrey began working in TV and radio while still in her teens. She never stopped. She is the exact opposite of lazy.

Winfrey revolutionized daytime TV, formed her own production company, wrote bestselling books, went into radio, starred in and produced films and then turned to Broadway.

You and Winfrey have more in common than you might believe. You both have something inside you that is a door to greatness. Winfrey found hers and used it. Will you do the same?

CHAPTER TWO

THE GOOD NEWS

"A pessimist sees the difficulty in every opportunity; an optimist sees the opportunity in every difficulty."
— WINSTON CHURCHILL

"Once you choose hope, anything's possible."
— CHRISTOPHER REEVE

"An optimist is someone who figures that if it walks like a duck and quacks like a duck, it's the bluebird of happiness."
— ROBERT BRAULT

"This is how humans are: We question all our beliefs, except for the ones we really believe, and those we never think to question."
— ORSON SCOTT CARD

WELCOME TO THE CLUB

So you're lazy.

Don't feel bad or guilty or hopeless because you're lazy. Be happy you're lazy! Thank God you're lazy!

It's a problem, but not that big of a problem.

* If laziness were something you were born with, that would be a huge problem.

* If laziness were the whole you, that would be a huge problem.

* If laziness were a bacterial disease, that would be a huge problem.

But it's not any of these things.

Laziness is a belief system. It's something you started saying about yourself. It's just a habit you've developed.

Do you realize that it takes only a flimsy rope to keep an elephant from running away? That's because when they are babies, elephants are tied with a strong rope. They're not strong enough to break away, and they stop trying. As adults, the elephants are much more powerful than the rope, but they don't know it. They are conditioned not to act.

Habits start off as thin threads and end up as strong cables. If your habit is a thin thread, this book will help you. If it's a strong cable, this book is essential.

The thing you call laziness is the result of poor choices. Or poor habits. It's not a genetic disorder. It's not a life sentence to failure. You're just lazy. And that's good news!

SEX. NOW THAT WE HAVE YOUR ATTENTION

The problem with laziness is that there's no drama to it. If you look at the talk shows on TV, you'll never see a show on laziness. Why? Because it's not exciting. It's not sexy or exotic.

But it is the killer disease of your professional and personal life. Laziness will keep you from graduating. It will keep you from getting promoted. It can destroy your marriage.

And do you know what the worst part of it is? You can't blame it on a disease that arrived in a ship's cargo hold. You can't blame it on a bad diet. You can't blame it on a powerful ray brought by aliens from outer space.

You know who the culprit is. It's you. But you also know who the hero of this story can be. It's you. You are the one who can stop being lazy.

Don't bother to watch "Oprah" or any of the self-help shows. The answer is within you.

Remember "The Wizard of Oz?" Dorothy wanted to get home. The scarecrow longed for a brain. The tin man wanted a heart. The cowardly lion cried for courage.

When they finally made it to Oz, the wizard helped all of them understand that they already had what they needed inside them.

It's the same way with you. Everything you need is already inside you.

"The time will come when winter will ask you what you were doing all summer." — Henry Clay

THE MOST DANGEROUS EPIDEMIC

If you ever find yourself with $4 million you don't know what to do with, you can buy one commercial – one – for the Super Bowl.

That's the estimated tab for a spot in the 2013 NFL title game. You may wonder why a single spot costs so much. That's easy – everybody is watching.

That's the problem with a lot of things. Everybody's watching. There are more than 100 million people watching the Super Bowl and only about 80 people playing in it. There's one person on stage at Carnegie Hall, with hundreds of people in the seats. It's an epidemic that's getting worse!

No wonder we're so lazy! We've even enshrined our laziness with a Super Bowl party. We get together and we munch chips while we watch. The closest we get to any kind of participation is filling out the form for the office pool.

Our entire culture feeds the laziness of being a spectator. We don't have to go out and buy the pizza; it gets delivered to our home. We can do our banking without getting out of the car, or even without leaving the house. We can change the channel on the TV while sitting on the couch.

No one could blame you for staying lazy. But you don't really want to be that way. Remember: There's a part of you that really wants to stop being lazy. The good news is that you can make this change any time you want.

UNLAZY HALL OF FAME
Capt. Sully Sullenberger

When pilot Capt. C.B. (Sully) Sullenberger took off on Jan. 15, 2009, he was doing something he had done thousands of times. Apparently, though, his flights had never become so routine that he stopped learning.

He knew just what to do when US Airways Flight 1549 lost power shortly after leaving New York's LaGuardia Airport. Sullenberger guided the airliner to a ditched landing in the Hudson River, saving 155 lives.

Interviewed by television news anchor Katie Couric, Sullenberger explained how he was able to perform with such skill under pressure.

He told her, "One way of looking at this might be that for 42 years, I've been making small, regular deposits in this bank of experience, education and training. And on January 15 the balance was sufficient so that I could make a very large withdrawal."

Those words can become your guide. Whatever you're doing, whatever you're trying to accomplish, you can get there by making what Sullenberger called "small, regular deposits."

As with Sullenberger, the more deposits you make, the more will be available in your personal bank account when you need to make a withdrawal.

THE BEST INVITATION IN THE WORLD

Once upon a time, a family crossed the ocean in search of a new life. They had only a little money, so they paid the lowest fare and got the smallest cabin on the ship. There they stayed for the whole voyage, eating the meager snacks that they had brought aboard.

The only exception was their little boy, who snuck out of the cabin. A wonderland opened. He saw people swimming in the pool and eating sumptuous meals. Racing back to the cabin, he told mom and dad about what he had seen, but they stayed where they were.

They never understood that their low-fare ticket gave them the same rights as everyone else! The food, the pool and all the attractions were there for them.

You're just like that family. You hold a ticket that entitles you to the banquets. The only question is whether you're going to attend. To do that, you have to leave your cabin and explore.

Somewhere inside you is a talent or an interest waiting to be discovered. Somewhere inside you is something that can fascinate you for the rest of your life.

Until you find that one thing, people may call you lazy. You may call yourself lazy. But you're not! You just haven't found the one thing that will bring out the energy within.

It can only happen if you leave your cabin and see what's on the other decks. Once you do that, the voyage will really begin!

CHAPTER THREE

THE CURE

"How wonderful it is that nobody need wait a single moment before starting to improve the world." — ANNE FRANK

"There are really only two requirements when it comes to exercise. One is that you do it. The other is that you continue to do it." — JENNIE BRAND-MILLER

"Movement is a medicine for creating change in a person's physical, emotional, and mental states." — CAROL WELCH

"Don't be fooled by the calendar. There are only as many days in the year as you make use of." — CHARLES RICHARDS

THE SHORTEST SEMINAR EVER

What is the absolute best way to motivate yourself? Reading won't do it. Words won't do it. Actions will. Your actions will change your attitudes, your motions will change your emotions, and your movements will change your moods.

Here's a story:

Many years ago, Nobel Prize-winning novelist Sinclair Lewis was scheduled to give an all-day writing seminar for college students.

Lewis began with a simple question: "How many of you really want to be writers?"

All the students in the room raised their hands.

After slowly looking around, Lewis packed up his briefcase and said, "In that case, my advice to you is to go home and write."

And with that, the great Sinclair Lewis left!

This famous writer knew the secret. You can think about writing, you can talk about writing, you can attend seminars on writing, but if you really want to be a writer, you have to write. Very simply, writers must write.

Nothing will motivate you as quickly and effectively as taking action.

THE INSTANT CURE

The cure for laziness is so simple you would scarcely believe it. But you have to believe it because you proved it by getting out of bed this morning.

You didn't feel like getting up, but you did. You felt one way but you acted another way.

This is the instant cure for laziness. You can act differently than you feel. You can feel like staying in bed, but still get up.

You can feel like skipping class or work, but you can go anyway.

You don't have to feel like writing in order to write. You don't have to feel like studying in order to study.

The biggest decision in your life is whether your feelings or your actions will be in charge.

Remember this rule:

Your feelings determine what you want.
Your actions determine what you'll get.

GET OFF YOUR ANATOMY

It turns out that getting people to see the cure for laziness takes a lot of $20 bills.

Now and then, to make a point in his speaking engagements, Dr. Gilbert takes a $20 bill from his pocket, holds it in the air and says, "Who wants this?" Hands go up and people yell out, "I do! I do!"

Dr. Gilbert's next question is, "Who *really* wants this money?" The hands go higher and the yells get louder.

And then Dr. Gilbert waits ... until eventually someone jumps out of his or her chair, runs to the front of the room and grabs the bill from his hand.

What, you may ask, is the point of this little game?

The person who gets the money demonstrates an important principle of success:

G.O.Y.A.

The acronym **G.O.Y.A.** stands for <u>G</u>et <u>O</u>ff <u>Y</u>our <u>A</u>natomy.

Just about every person in that room wanted, wished, desired and hoped to get that money. The money went to the person who *got off his/her anatomy* and took action.

Winston Churchill, the statesman who led Great Britain through World War II, said, "I never worry about action, but only inaction." Be like Winston Churchill. Make inaction a thing you can't tolerate.

UNLAZY HALL OF FAME
Mother Teresa

Mother Teresa was a Roman Catholic nun who spent most of her life tending to the poor in the dirtiest slums of Calcutta, India. She brought hope and help to thousands of people. Today she is viewed as a worldwide symbol of service to others.

What could anyone possibly have in common with Mother Teresa? Plenty.

It was revealed not long after her death that for much of her life, Mother Teresa lived with deep spiritual doubts. Even though she belonged to a religious order, she went years at a time in a crisis of faith.

In that respect, Mother Teresa was like million of others who live with doubts. Here's what separates her from those millions: She never let her feelings interfere with her actions.

When Mother Teresa felt spiritual emptiness, she still tended to the sick. When she felt spiritual darkness, she did not go on vacation to a glamorous beach. She stayed in the most unglamorous of settings, in Calcutta with the people who desperately needed her help. Few people – if any – knew what Mother Teresa was feeling. They knew only what she was doing.

That's how you can be like Mother Teresa. As you go through life, there will be plenty of days when you just don't feel like doing what you're called upon to do. On those days, you can either give in to the feelings, or you can act differently than you feel.

THE FIVE KILLER WORDS

Suppose you could look at your life as a big bag of sand. Each grain would represent one minute of your time here on Earth.

Then imagine the sand would be poured into one of two bowls. One would hold all the action grains: the minutes in which you worked, studied, took a risk, got out of your comfort zone. The other would hold all the "I-don't-feel-like-it" grains:

I don't feel like studying.

I don't feel like trying.

I don't feel like getting out of bed.

Which bowl would hold more sand? Every grain in the "I-don't-feel-like-it" bag stands for a missed opportunity and, even worse, for a question that neither you nor anyone else will ever be able to answer.

What if you had gotten out of bed?

What if you had tried just a little harder?

What if you had been a bit more persistent?

Every moment you have a choice between doing it and not doing it. Your life will change the instant you stop letting The Five Killer Words – "I don't feel like it" – poison your dreams.

DETERMINED TO BE LAZY!
(Coach Tully speaking)

When I told a group of students that it was good news that they were lazy, they asked why.

"If you lacked skill," I told them, "it would be a huge problem. It takes a long time to build skill. But if you're lazy, you can fix that problem in a moment."

They didn't like that answer. "But what if we're determined to be lazy?"

There's no such thing as being determined to be lazy. Being determined is the exact opposite of being lazy.

Being determined is about energy. Being lazy is about lack of energy. Determination is a strength word; laziness is a weakness word.

Determination has helped millions of people become successful. Laziness has never helped anyone do anything.

So if you're determined, you've got energy, strength and action on your side. It's an unbeatable combination!

WHY HUMAN BEINGS AREN'T EXTINCT

Babies aren't born lazy. They're hard workers. The more you watch them, the more you see it.

Babies work hard to roll over. They work hard to sit up. They work hard to crawl, then to stand. They work hard to walk and will fall down and get up as many times as it takes. They work hard to talk, starting with one word, then with phrases, and finally with sentences.

If you've ever been a babysitter for a 2-year-old, you know exactly how unlazy they are. They'll climb stairs, chairs and sofas. You have to lock cabinets to make sure they won't open the doors and explore what's inside.

You were like this when you were a baby. Then somehow you stopped exploring and started playing it safe. Who knows when or why? But this ability to explore is still inside you, ready to be turned on with one decision.

If you were born without energy, it would be really bad news. There wouldn't be much that you – or anyone else – could do to make things better. But you weren't born without energy. You were born with intense curiosity about what's in the cabinet. You were born with the persistence that helped you walk and talk. The curiosity and persistence are there the minute you decide to channel them.

UNLAZY HALL OF FAME
Lou Costello

One night many years ago, Lou Costello went on the air for his weekly radio show with his comedy partner, Bud Abbott. To the audience, there seemed to be nothing different from all the other "Abbott & Costello" shows.

But the audience didn't know the story behind the story. Just hours before going on the air, Costello learned that his son – not yet two years old – had fallen into the family swimming pool and drowned.

That night Costello was a clown with a broken heart. He joked even when he felt like crying. He was just affirming a rule of success, no matter where you are in life: You can act differently than you feel.

There's a saying, "Act the way you want to become, and you will become the way you act."

Keep acting motivated until you feel motivated.
Keep acting excited until you feel excited.
Keep acting energized until you feel energized.

Right now, if you're an athlete and you're going to practice, your job is to **act** energized, excited and interested, even if you don't **feel** like it.

You might not be able to change your feelings right now, but you're always able to change your actions. And when you change your actions, your feelings will follow.

YOUR GREATEST COMPETITIVE EDGE

There's even more good news about you and laziness. You're not the only one who is lazy. Millions of other people are lazy, too.

Your competitors are lazy. Some people you admire are lazy. Even so-called winners are lazy.

Want proof? How many winning lottery tickets go unclaimed? How many scholarships go unused because no one will apply for them? How many people buy a gym membership but never go there to work out? How many musical instruments or exercise machines are sitting idle in the basement?

See? Your competition is lazy!

Famous singer Billy Joel was once asked the secret of his success. His answer shows exactly how much you can gain just by being a little bit more active than the next person.

We're paraphrasing, because the interview took place over the radio years ago, but Joel's thought went like this: I'm not the best songwriter, but I can write a song. I'm not the best singer, but I can sing a song. My band isn't the greatest band. But here's what we do. When we sign a contract for a concert and promise to be in a certain place at a certain time and play for a certain amount of time, we do it."

In other words, Billy Joel has created a great career by meeting minimum standards. That's not a knock on him or his talent. It's just a commentary on his competition – and yours!

UNLAZY HALL OF FAME
Melissa Sapio

Melissa Sapio took Billy Joel's formula a step further.

Sapio was a moderately successful high school student who made one adjustment when she enrolled in college. She decided that she would always do just a little more than expected.

If the professor told the class to read one chapter, Sapio would read two. If the assignment was to solve two math problems, she would solve three.

This small adjustment brought dramatic results. Sapio graduated with a perfect 4.0 average and is today a psychologist.

Some people might look at Sapio and be tempted to call her a genius. But she's not. She's just unlazy. She's also a reminder that no matter what you do in life, you have choices.

You can be lazy, like Dr. Gilbert was when it came time to pay his parking ticket.

You can be like Billy Joel, and do a great job of meeting expectations.

Or you can be like Melissa Sapio, exceeding expectations and producing dramatic results.

Your life will be the sum of the choices you make.

THE WRONG WAY TO CLEAN YOUR CAR

Comedienne Joan Rivers summed up domestic laziness with one quip. She said, "I hate housework. You make the beds and wash the floor, and six months later you have to start all over."

Here's the story of someone who got lazy with some cleaning, but there's nothing funny about the way things turned out.

A man was eating in his car and when he finished, he wanted to get rid of the bag. There was a garbage can not far from where the man was parked, but he was too lazy to open his car door, get out and walk to it.

He tried to toss the garbage into the can, but missed. He was too lazy to get out of the car and pick up the litter, so he left it there and drove away.

Later that day, the man got a call at his home. Someone had seen him leave the bag on the ground. Actually, it wasn't just someone. It was the mayor of the town. Now the man had to go through the hassle of paying the fine.

A little bit of laziness had cost him a lot in terms of time, trouble and money, to say nothing of the embarrassment of getting called out by the mayor.

There are much easier and more constructive ways to meet your local officials.

THE UNLAZY ALARM
(Dr. Gilbert Speaking)

When I was in graduate school in a residence hall at UMass/ Amherst, I lived on the 19th floor of a 22-story building. By 10 p.m., I was exhausted and usually sleeping.

One night I was so tired I could hardly keep my eyes open. All of a sudden, the fire alarm went off and I smelled smoke. It didn't take a doctorate to know that there was trouble. I instantly became totally energized because I knew I had to take care of the residents and make sure everyone evacuated the building.

My energy level went from nothing to extremely high almost immediately. I instantly cured myself of my laziness. Well, that's not really true. Actually, it was the circumstances that cured me.

Here's the secret of this book: You don't have to wait for the circumstances to be just right before you act. There doesn't have to be a fire or other emergency. You can act right now, no matter what the circumstances are.

In fact, the more you act without waiting for the circumstances to be perfect, the more rewards will come to you.

Your life will come down to how you answer these two questions:

Are your circumstances stronger than you are?

Or are you stronger than your circumstances?

THE INSTANT CURE IN ACTION

It was Thursday night, a big party night on many college campuses. The student was at the library at about 8 p.m. studying for an exam he had to take the next day. After about 45 minutes of studying, he was so bored and discouraged he fell asleep over his books.

At about 9 p.m., one of his fraternity brothers found him sleeping, woke him up and told him about a party off campus. The next thing the student knew it was 3:30 in the morning and he was still partying.

He went from unenergized to energized pretty quickly. He cured his laziness instantly.

It wasn't that he was out of gas. His tank was full! He was unwilling to put the key into the ignition.

That all changed when it was time to party. He was more excited about the party than he was about the exam. The party made him put the key into the ignition.

Does this mean you should go through life looking for parties to motivate yourself?

Exactly the opposite.

Go through life with the knowledge that the energy is inside you, and you can activate it any time you want.

FROM *F* TO *A*

Here's a case study of two students from the fall semester of 2010. First there's Mary. She got an F the first time she took the Laziness Demonstration. The second time she got a higher F, but still an F. The third time she got a C and the fourth time she got an A for the Laziness Demonstration and an A for the course. She cured herself of laziness!

Then there's Johnny. He spent five hours taking the exam the first time. (There's no time limit.) He received a B. He retook the Laziness Demonstration and put in four more hours. He didn't improve his grade – a B again. He was mad. He was told that it isn't how much time you put in; it's what you put into the time. He wasn't receptive. He never retook the Laziness Demonstration and received a B for the Laziness Demonstration – and for the course.

He probably thought that the professor was unreasonable or that the professor didn't like him or that the professor played favorites.

Remember **RATIONAL LIES**? He was telling himself **RATIONAL LIES**.

The reason Johnny got a B is he was too lazy to study more and retake the Laziness Demonstration. Mary wasn't lazy. She kept taking the test until she got an A.

Mary was no smarter than Johnny. She was just unlazy.

WHERE WE UNCOVERED THE INSTANT CURE

Frank Bettger was a young man who dreamed of becoming a big-league baseball player. Then one day he was cut from the team. He asked the manager why, and the answer changed his life.

"You walk around the field like an old man," the manager told him. "You have no energy."

Most people would have walked away from the game, bitter at the rejection. Frank Bettger took the feedback to heart. He vowed that on his next team he would be the most energetic player on the field. He made sure that no one could out-hustle him.

Sure enough, Bettger reached his dream of playing in the big leagues. He lasted only a part of one season, but at least he learned that a person can always act energized, and Bettger made sure that he always did.

More important, Bettger used his new attitude and showed that same energy in his career after baseball. He wrote the best-selling book "How I Raised Myself from Failure to Success in Selling."

Bettger changed his life by changing his attitude. He did it in a moment. You can do the same thing and become the next Frank Bettger. Don't ever give anyone the chance to say that you lack energy and hustle. The minute you start making sure that no one out-hustles you, miracles begin.

Maybe it won't be in baseball or sales. It doesn't have to be. Just start showing so much passion in your field that no one could ever miss it.

THE SECRET OF LIFE...
JUST THREE WORDS

If you check out your life, an instant cure for laziness has been there all the time.

It's three words (four if you count the contraction): It's about others.

If you want to instantly energize, activate or inspire yourself, do something for somebody else.

If you want to get motivated, motivate somebody else. If you want to be happy, make someone else happy. If you want to become unlazy, help somebody else become unlazy.

If you're unhappy, buy a present for someone else. You'll become happy in the giving.

When you think about it, these three (or four) words apply to a lot of life.

It's about others.

Basketball coach John Wooden said, "You can't live a perfect day until you do something for someone who will never be able to repay you."

It's a beautiful sentiment, though not quite true. Every good deed you do for another is actually good for you, too. Focus on someone else and the byproduct will be good feelings about yourself.

TIME TO GET EXCITED

We are born excited about life, but we lose this feeling somewhere along the way.

If you've ever been out for a walk with a 2-year-old, you know that a single trip around the block can last nearly an hour.

Children want to see everything. They lie flat on their bellies, heads propped up in their hands, to watch ants criss-cross the sidewalk. They notice the birds and hear them sing. They ask questions. They pause on their walk. They even retrace steps to explore something they noticed along the way.

For every child with this kind of curiosity, there is a parent who must hurry for an appointment or get home to make dinner. When the parent wants to hurry, the child has no choice but to go along.

But you have a choice! You can linger and marvel at the ants. You can listen to the birds or dip your toe into a stream. There are a million things to get excited about!

Remember, you don't have to get interested in **everything**. You just have to get interested in **something**. When you find that something, you will be shocked at how quickly you become unlazy.

DON'T LET THIS HAPPEN TO YOU

One day Dr. Gilbert walked into class and asked the students a question. "Is anyone doing anything exciting this week?"

One person raised his hand to say that, yes, he was doing something exciting. In fact, he was looking at the chance of a lifetime. He had received a call from an agent about appearing as an extra in a movie directed by Woody Allen.

His agent told him to go to a certain place at a certain time, where a bus would take him and the other extras to the set – which was in a secret location.

When the student returned to class a few days later, everyone wanted to know how the filming had gone. Instead, he offered only two words: "I overslept."

Then he added ... "And I don't want to talk about it."

No wonder he didn't want to talk about it. He had blown the chance of a lifetime by failing to meet the minimum expectations. Remember Billy Joel in a previous story? Joel climbed to the top of the music world simply by delivering on the promises he makes.

There's a saying that when people look back over their lives, they don't regret the things they did as much as the things they didn't do.

You certainly don't want to be looking back one day and summing up your life with these two words: "I overslept."

SUGAR, SUGAR, SUGAR

Here's a quote on a T-shirt worn by a college student: "You can always retake the course, but you'll never be able to make up the party."

Funny quote, but dangerous advice! *To be successful, you've got to tend to what's important.* If you're a college student, it's important to fight through the temptation to go to that party. You have to fight through wanting to stay in bed when it's time for class. You have to fight through senioritis and spring fever when you would much prefer to be outside playing Frisbee.

You've got to delay gratification. You've got to do what you **must** before you do what you **want**. Business before pleasure.

Years ago, researchers used young children and some M&M candy to study delayed gratification. They placed a child in a room alone at a table. Then they set four or five M&Ms on the table.

"You can eat the M&Ms any time you want," said the researchers. "But if you can wait until we come back, you can have even more M&Ms."

Retiring behind a wall, the researchers watched the children attempt to cope. They tried a variety of strategies to avoid eating the sweets. Some placed their hands in their lap. Others looked away. Some gave in to the temptation and gobbled the candy.

Researchers followed the children for years, and found that those who were able to delay gratification fared better in life. So can you!

ARE YOU PREJUDICED?

Most people don't think of themselves as prejudiced. They would get insulted if you told them they were. But many people have an extremely destructive form of prejudice. It's prejudice against themselves! They prejudge who and what they are, and wind up rejecting themselves.

Look, there are plenty of people in this world who will reject you. If you're a student, a college can reject you. If you're in sales, the client can walk away. If you ask someone for a date, he or she can tell you to get lost.

But let them do the rejecting! Don't reject yourself before you even try. That's what people are really doing when they call themselves lazy. They're rejecting themselves before someone else can.

These people are putting themselves in a kind of box. It's a self-imposed limitation. They say they're lazy when in fact they just don't feel like it, aren't interested, are unmotivated, bored or shy.

Dr. Gilbert once knew a student in the process of applying to college. When Dr. Gilbert asked where she wanted to go, she told him Columbia. He asked her if she had applied. She hadn't, because she didn't think Columbia would accept her.

She had rejected herself.

With Dr. Gilbert's help, she applied. She got in.

There is no guarantee that you will get into your dream situation just because you apply. But it's a guarantee that you'll never get in if you don't try. Don't be prejudiced against yourself.

CHAPTER FOUR

YOUR POTENTIAL

"I'd rather be partly great than entirely useless." — NEIL SHUSTERMAN

"Every day, people settle for less than they deserve." — BO BENNETT

"The potential of the average person is like a huge ocean unsailed." — BRIAN TRACY

"In all realms of life it takes courage to stretch your limits, express your power and fulfill your potential." — SUZE ORMAN

"Opportunities multiply as they are seized." — SUN TZU

"Potential has a shelf life." — MARGARET ATWOOD

WHAT YOU DON'T KNOW ABOUT TOM CRUISE

There are three parts of you:

1. The things you know about yourself.

2. The things you don't know about yourself.

3. The things you don't know you don't know about yourself.

No. 3 is where the gold is. It's where your hidden treasure resides. It's where an undiscovered talent is.

Once there was a high school athlete who was on the sidelines with an injury. Rather than do nothing, he decided to try out for the school play. To his surprise, he not only got a part, he got the male lead.

Meanwhile, the mother of one of the performers was a real stage mom. She always wanted an agent in the audience to see her child in action. Sure enough, the agent was there the night of the play. The agent didn't see much in the stage mom's child, but he thought the young man had potential.

The rest is history. The young man's name was Tom Cruise, and his performance launched a career in show business.

There are two morals to this story. First, like the young Tom Cruise, you have people – teachers, mentors, coaches or agents – who may see something in you. They can see things about you that you don't see in yourself.

Second, whenever you take action, forces in the universe tend to get on your side. The injury, the mom and the agent were forces that converged to help Cruise. But nothing would have happened if he had stayed on the sidelines.

YOU ARE A MARVEL

When you say, "I am lazy," it means that you're not using your potential. When you say, "I'm not smart," it means that you think you don't have the potential. Never think you don't have the potential. You are a marvel.

If you don't want to believe us, listen to the words of legendary Spanish cellist Pablo Casals:

"And what do we teach our children in school? We teach them that two and two make four and that Paris is the capital of France. When will we also teach them what they are? You should say to each of them: You are unique. In all the world there is no other child exactly like you. In the millions of years that have passed there has never been a child like you. And look at your body – what a wonder it is! Your legs, your arms, your cunning fingers, the way you move! You may be a Shakespeare, a Michelangelo, a Beethoven. You have the capacity for anything. Yes, you are a marvel."

Some people feel they can never be a marvel because they can't write like Shakespeare, sculpt like Michelangelo or compose like Beethoven. Don't let that bother you! You don't have to produce the same product that those legends did. You just have to be like them in one way: Go where the road takes you.

Each day the world presents more and more roads for you to explore. There are diseases to be cured, businesses to be started, products to be developed. The computer age lets you succeed in ways that you never dreamed!

It's all possible ... because you are a marvel!

APPLES AND SEEDS

QUESTION 1: Suppose we gave you an apple and a knife. Could you cut up the apple and count the number of *seeds* in the *apple*?

Of course you could – that's just a persistence task.

QUESTION 2: Now suppose we gave you just one of the seeds. Could you count the number of *apples* in a *seed*?

Anyone can count the number of seeds in an apple. No one can count the number of apples in the seed.

This book is not about fruit – it's about your potential.

Did you ever hear of baseball player Mike Piazza? He is one of the top players in history, a sure bet for the Hall of Fame.

But years ago when baseball held its annual draft of high school players, no one looked at Piazza as a Hall of Famer. They scarcely looked at him at all!

In the first round of the draft, every team ignored Piazza. The same thing happened in the second round. It wasn't until 1,398 players had been chosen that the Los Angeles Dodgers finally took a chance on Piazza. It turned out to be one of the best picks they ever made.

Chances are that you won't be the same kind of player that Piazza was. But you have gifts that no one has seen yet. That's because maybe you haven't seen them yet. Start looking!

YOUR PAST IS NOT YOUR FUTURE

A common mistake is to confuse your past with your future. For example, "I didn't do well in high school so I won't do well in college."

Don't limit yourself like that. <u>Your past is NOT your future</u>. What would happen if you drove your car by looking only in the rear-view mirror? Looking only at where you <u>have been</u> creates accidents.

YOUR PAST IS NOT YOUR POTENTIAL.

REPEAT: YOUR PAST <u>IS NOT</u> YOUR POTENTIAL.

But ... your focus is your future. Don't focus on your past results – focus on your potential.

When Dr. Gilbert speaks to large groups, he sometimes uses the "right hand" experiment to show people the difference between their performance and their potential.

He gets his volunteers to stand near a wall and gives them a marker. He then asks them to jump as high as possible and put a mark on the wall. Next he asks if they can jump any higher. They say, "a little bit, but not much."

That's when Dr. Gilbert takes a $20 bill from his wallet and tapes it to the wall, four inches higher than the original mark.

Miraculously, the volunteers always jump not just a little bit higher, but a lot higher!

There's a big difference between what you're doing now and what you can do in the future.

"Never underestimate
the power of dreams
and the influence of
the human spirit. We
are all the same in this
notion: The potential
for greatness lives
within each of us." —
WILMA RUDOLPH

UNLAZY HALL OF FAME
Blanche Rudolph

In the 1940s, life was tough for millions of Americans, particularly blacks in the South like Blanche Rudolph.

Besides working as a maid and making her children's clothes out of flour sacks, she found time to tend to her daughter Wilma, who had developed polio.

Twice a week for two years, Blanche Rudolph took Wilma to a non-segregated clinic 50 miles away. She also learned the physical therapy techniques and the exercises that would help Wilma at home.

By the time Wilma reached 12, Blanche's efforts had paid off. Wilma could walk normally. In fact, she moved well enough to go out for basketball. There she was discovered by Ed Temple, coach of the women's track team at Tennessee State. Temple had found one of America's greatest sprinters.

Wilma attended college on scholarship, then qualified for the Olympics. She captured a bronze medal in 1956, and four years later became the first American woman to win three golds.

From polio to Olympic champion! The story defies belief, except that it's right there in the record books. But that's the way life is. The bigger the problem, the greater the glory. None of it would have been possible without Blanche Rudolph, Wilma's unlazy mother.

THE UNLAZY GAME

Think about certain people you knew in high school. There was probably someone who wasn't very good at memorizing Spanish vocabulary or learning important dates in history. Poor memory? No. This person knew every sports statistic by heart.

Don't confuse poor memory with lack of interest. Interest ignites the memory. Boredom douses/stomps out memory.

Then there's the student who couldn't memorize a poem, but who could effortlessly remember *Ya Got Trouble* from "The Music Man" or the entire collection of The Beatles.

Poor memory? No. Poor motivation? Absolutely!!!

You've experienced this in your own life. When you're excited to tell someone about a movie or a concert you attended, you can remember every detail.

When you're this excited, can you imagine having to say, "I don't remember?" No way.

If you're not learning, don't blame it on a poor memory. You've got all the ability in the world. You're just not interested enough to use it.

Here's how to get interested when you're really not. Invent a little game to help you remember things. Use rhymes or songs. Make up stories. Take notes in different shapes or colors. The only limit is your imagination. When you play this game, you'll get interested instead of bored, and you'll amaze yourself with what you can remember.

SEEING WHAT'S THERE

The next time you see a FedEx truck or envelope, try to find the arrow. You may have to look a little while before you see it. It's right there between the second E and the X. Once you see this arrow for the first time, you won't be able to miss it again.

Now that you know about the arrow, what about the spoon? You've probably never seen that one, either, but it's right there in the bottom half of the first E.

The FedEx logo is a lot like life: There are always things you haven't seen. There are always situations in search of solutions. There are treasures waiting to be discovered.

Acres of Diamonds by Russell H. Conwell tells of a man who saw a shiny rock in a garden stream, brought it into his house and placed it on his mantel. He forgot about it until a visitor noticed it and said it was a diamond!

They went out to the garden stream, where they found more of the gems. They had discovered the legendary mines of Golconda!

All the while, the man had a fortune sitting right under his eyes, and he never even knew it. He didn't see the arrow or the spoon in the FedEx logo.

There are opportunities around you every day, whether you see them or not. One way to see them is to believe that they are there, and to start looking for them.

Don't put a gem on your mantel and just forget about it!

HOW ON EARTH DO YOU KNOW?

Do you realize that one of the most puzzling questions in modern science revolves around you?

It's true! Scientists want to know if you're going to be a success.

They are trying to answer the same question that stumps colleges, sports teams and bosses: Which of their many candidates will turn out well, and which ones will fail?

If you're successful, scientists will want to learn why. If you're not, they will want to know more about that, too.

So far, no one has come up with a perfect way to help people select the right candidate.

Here's a question for you: If the greatest researchers in the world don't know if you're going to be a success, what makes you so sure you won't be?

Too many people go through life believing that success belongs to someone else. They hear motivational stories about how the underdog won, but they seldom see themselves as the hero in those stories.

Those stories can be about you! Find something that gets you off the couch. Years from now, one of those researchers might be interviewing you to learn the secret of your success!

CHAPTER FIVE

THE STRATEGIES

"To change one's life: Start immediately. Do it flamboyantly. No exceptions."
— WILLIAM JAMES

"Why always 'not yet?' Do flowers in spring say 'not yet'"? — NORMAN DOUGLAS

"Don't look where you fall, but where you slipped." — AFRICAN PROVERB

"One may walk over the highest mountain one step at a time." — JOHN WANAMAKER

"To hell with circumstances; I create opportunities." — BRUCE LEE

"Every saint has a past. Every sinner has a future." — UNKNOWN

LIFE'S MOST IMPORTANT RIDDLE

Three frogs were sitting on a log. One decided to jump off. How many frogs were left on the log?

Most people say two. But it's a trick question, and we don't know the answer. It could either be two or three.

Why?

Just because the frog decided to jump doesn't mean that he actually did.

Same way with you. There's a big gap between deciding and doing. You don't become successful just by deciding. You have to back up your deciding with doing.

In this chapter, we'll give you strategies to help you close the gap between deciding and doing. They can help you get unlazy. You don't have to use all of them. But one of them is going to strike you as the right one.

You don't want to be left on the log when the rest of the frogs jump into the water.

Following are 10 proven strategies for getting unlazy in a hurry:

1. FIND A BIG ENOUGH REASON

Years ago a man named Randy Leamer learned that his daughter had a problem with one of her kidneys.

Without a transplant, she would die. Doctors looked for a donor, but they couldn't find the perfect match – except for Leamer himself.

There was just one problem. Leamer was grossly overweight and doctors wouldn't operate on him. They couldn't take the chance, and they told him so.

Time was running short, so Leamer asked the doctors, "How much weight do I have to lose?"

A hundred pounds, they told him.

Within six months, Leamer lost the hundred pounds. The doctors went ahead with the operation, and his daughter was saved.

His daughter's illness did for Leamer what nothing else could do: motivate him to lose weight.

Vanity didn't help.

Health reasons didn't help.

The only thing that helped Leamer was the knowledge that without his kidney, his daughter would die.

He had found the reason. If you want to get unlazy, find a big enough reason.

2. LISTEN TO SIR ISAAC NEWTON

Sir Isaac Newton knew the power of getting started. One of his Laws of Motion holds that a body in motion tends to stay in motion.

So if you want to get going, then get going. The secret of getting started is getting started.

Remember the acronym **ACE**:
Action **C**reates **E**xcitement.
Action **C**reates **E**nthusiasm.
Action **C**reates **E**nergy.

If you're not excited – act excited.
If you're not enthused – act enthused.
If you're not energized – act energized.

Maybe you've heard the maxim, "Fake it 'til you make it." Good advice. You should also "Fake it 'til you *feel* it." Once you put your body in motion, the emotions will follow.

If you wait until you *feel* like doing something, you might never do it. But, once you start doing it, you're more likely to feel like doing it.

Here's another acronym for **ACE**:

Action **C**ures **E**verything.

Especially laziness. Try the cure today. It was prescribed by Sir Isaac Newton!

3. HANG AROUND WITH UNLAZY PEOPLE
(Dr. Gilbert Speaking)

I'm always an easy grader. In my Freshman Seminar classes, I'm an even easier grader. It's almost impossible to fail that course, but this student did. Years later I ran into him and he gave me a big greeting.

That was funny in itself because usually people give me a big hello only if they've done well in my class. If they didn't do well, they ignore me.

"Dr. Gilbert, I bet you don't remember me," he said.

"I don't remember your name but I remember you flunked Freshman Seminar," I said. "What are you doing now?"

"I graduated and am going to medical school," he said.

"How?" I wanted to know. How was such a thing possible?

"Right after I took your class," the student explained, "I went to a party and met the girl I'm now engaged to. I just wanted to hang out with her, and she studied a lot. So I studied a lot. Now it's four years later and we're both going to medical school."

This student became unlazy in the easiest way possible. He began hanging around with someone who wasn't lazy. If you want to become a better tennis player, start hanging around with better tennis players. If you want to be a better student, start hanging around with better students.

You will become unlazy in no time.

4. FOLLOW COACH GELSTON'S ONLY RULE

Ollie Gelston coached basketball for many years at Montclair State University in northern New Jersey.

Every year in the middle of October, he greeted the new crop of players.

"You've all come from different high schools," he would say. "You've had different coaches and different rules, so I will make this simple."

He then gave them his rule. His only rule.

Be in the **right place**, at the **right time**, and do the **right thing**.

It was pure genius. These were college students, and they weren't stupid.

They knew what the right **place** was.

They knew what the right **time** was.

They knew what the right **thing** was.

Coach Gelston's rule isn't just for basketball players. It's for everyone.

You know what the right **place** is.

You know what the right **time** is.

You know what the right **thing** is.

Coach Gelston made it simple. Just follow his rule!

5. IMAGINE YOUR WAY TO SUCCESS

Have you ever had a nightmare? You probably have. You woke up in a sweat with your heart pounding.

There's a scientific reason for that physical reaction. Dr. Maxwell Maltz, author of *Psycho-Cybernetics*, made the point that the subconscious mind does not know the difference between a real experience and one that is vividly imagined.

Successful people use this principle all the time. Golfers visualize the path of the ball before they hit it. Skiers imagine going through the twists and turns before they fly down the mountain.

You can imagine yourself being successful. See yourself in a new car, or taking a vacation to your dream destination.

The more vividly you imagine the scene, the more likely it will come to pass. You will motivate yourself to take the necessary action.

But, you protest, you've often thought about driving that new car and nothing happened. Yes, you've **THOUGHT** about it. But you did not **VIVIDLY IMAGINE** it.

There's a big difference between the two, a difference that can take you from lazy to unlazy, from the couch to the winner's circle, from regrets to fulfillment.

6. MAKE A BET

One year, Dr. Gilbert asked his classes for feedback on the semester. Most of the comments were favorable, but some students mentioned a distraction: Dr. Gilbert was always asking what time it was.

Determined that he would never again distract the class in this way, Dr. Gilbert made a bet with his students. He said that if they ever caught him without a watch, he would pay them $100.

There were no hitches. Before class, after class, in the hallways, on the quad, anywhere! And to make sure that he would never have to pay up, Dr. Gilbert went out and got three or four watches!

The bet gave Dr. Gilbert the motivation he needed, and a bet can help you, too!

One time, Coach Tully and a co-worker were both trying to lose weight. Nothing seemed to help either one of them. Finally they made a bet with each other that went like this:

If you don't make your target weight by the target date, **you** have to treat **me** to a round-trip flight anywhere in the continental United States.

With stakes that high, Coach Tully and his co-worker both found the motivation to lose the weight by the target date.

Try this technique! You can bet someone that you will wake up at a certain time every morning, that you will work out on a given day, that you will finish a project on time, or anything else where laziness is holding you back!

7. GET A PEN AND AN INDEX CARD

Milt Campbell ranks among the greatest athletes in U.S. history, having won an Olympic gold medal in decathlon and then playing in the National Football League.

As a motivational speaker, he would challenge his audiences to think about goal-setting. He would inquire, "How many of you have goals?" All the hands would go up. Then Campbell would ask, "How many of you have written down your goals?" Not quite as many hands would go up. Finally he would ask, "How many of you have your goals with you right now?" Hardly any hands went up at all.

Looking at your goals every day helps you connect what you **want** with what you **do**. By keeping your goals where you can see them daily, you increase your chances of doing what's necessary.

It's said that Campbell's advice influenced Dan O'Brien, who won an Olympic decathlon gold in 1996. Now a motivational speaker in his own right, O'Brien spreads the message of setting goals.

We're not saying that O'Brien's goal-setting techniques were the whole reason for his success in international sports.

But we're saying that without some daily connection to your dreams, you will never take the action needed to make them come true.

.

8. PAY ME NOW OR PAY ME LATER

Media personality Larry King was long hooked on cigarettes. He tried to help himself, without success. The listeners to his late-night radio show called in with advice, but nothing seemed to work.

King's actions changed in a hurry the day he had a heart attack. Scared for his life, he never let another cigarette touch his lips.

He also changed his diet. He felt that missing out on the taste of pizza or steak was nothing compared to going through more heart surgery. But it took a heart attack to make him feel that way. Advice didn't help. Neither did warnings from the Surgeon General.

The moral for you is that if the little things don't motivate you, the big things will.

King's case brings to mind the old commercial for Fram oil filters. The message was that you can either buy an auto filter today for a small price, or rebuild your engine later for a huge price.

"You can pay me now, or pay me later," was the message.

The choice is yours.

How about you? Will you get motivated now? Or will you wait until later?

9. STOP TRYING

In sales they say, "Trying is lying."

In "The Empire Strikes Back," Yoda tells Luke Skywalker, "Do or do not, there is no try."

There's no payoff for the things you try to do. The payoff comes from the things you actually do.

Imagine yourself on a high diving board. You can either jump or not jump. But you can't *try* to jump. Once you climb that ladder, you either wind up in the water or you climb back down.

There are only two kinds of people: those who do and those who don't.

Those who do, do. Those who don't, don't.

There are those who get results and those who always have reasons for why they don't get results.

Stop trying and start doing.

Remember these nine words: Cowards don't begin. Losers don't finish. Winners don't quit.

10. USE FRANK SOMMA'S FORMULA

Frank Somma has one of the toughest jobs in the world. He's a sales trainer. The great thing about sales is that if you're unlazy, you can make incredible amounts of money. The bad news is that if you are lazy, you'll starve.

At his training sessions, Somma talks about going from inaction to action. He puts it into three steps:

1. Make a commitment.
2. Make it public.
3. Make it happen.

If you want a commitment to mean something, don't make it in private, do it in public. Most people don't get married in private. They invite guests and they make their vows in public.

It's the same way with your projects. If you have to make 50 sales calls today, tell someone. The peer pressure will make it more likely that you will follow through.

If you need to work out five times a week, make it public. If you're going to an audition, let as many people as possible know.

Whenever you're tempted to be lazy at anything, make a commitment, make it public and make it happen.

CHAPTER SIX

URGENCY

"You may delay, but time will not."
— BENJAMIN FRANKLIN

"How we spend our days is, of course, how we spend our lives." — ANNIE DILLARD

"Most of us spend our lives as if we had another one in the bank." — BEN IRWIN

"Every day of our lives we are on the verge of making those slight changes that would make all the difference."
— MIGNON McLAUGHLIN

"Study the past if you would define the future."
— CONFUCIUS

PROCRASTINATION

Somebody once defined procrastination as getting ready to get ready.

Most people die with their songs unsung.

After one Civil War battle, a review of the field showed that many of the muskets had not been fired! The soldiers had weapons and ammo, but had not used them.

There's only one way to avoid all that waste: Start acting unlazy right now.

Notice that we said start *acting* unlazy.

It's OK to *feel* lazy. Everybody does. But it's not OK to *act* lazy.

There's a lesson that armies can teach about crossing rivers. When you reach one in the evening, cross it. You may not feel like it after a long day of marching, but if you wait until the morning, the chance may be gone. There may be floods, high tides or bad weather.

There's a bridge in your life right now. You don't feel like crossing it, but there's an opportunity that may not be there tomorrow. Cross now while you can.

It's later than you think. What are you waiting for? Don't *get ready* to start doing what you have to do. START DOING WHAT YOU HAVE TO!!! Don't let the start stop you.

THE BRIDGE YOU MUST CROSS

Baseball Hall of Famer Ty Cobb practiced like few players ever have. When he went into a batting slump, he attacked the problem with hours of focused practice.

Cobb placed a towel on a strategic part of the field, then took batting practice until he could hit the ball directly to the towel. It took hundreds of balls.

Who knows what Cobb's teammates were doing while this exercise was taking place? Maybe playing cards in the clubhouse? Making fun of Cobb? Whatever they were doing, it certainly wasn't what Cobb was doing.

Here are two crucial questions for you. First, COULD you practice the way Cobb did? Yes, you could. But WILL you practice that way? That's a different question.

The point is: Life is not a game of can. It is a game of will. There's no doubt that you can. You can practice as hard as Ty Cobb. But will you?

Life's rewards don't go to those who can. Anyone can. The rewards go to those who will. You CAN get out of bed in the morning. But WILL you? You CAN eat a proper diet. But WILL you? You CAN delay gratification. But WILL you?

The more you think about life, the more you realize that success isn't something that happens to you. Success is something that you make happen.

You must cross the bridge between CAN and WILL.

DO YOU NEED THIS?

Gymnast Kerri Strug became a hero at the 1996 Olympics because she did what she needed to do when she needed to do it.

With her team locked in a very tight medal fight with Russia, Strug injured her ankle on a poorly executed vault.

While waiting for her next turn, she asked coach Bela Karolyi, "Do we need this?" In other words, did the U.S. medal depend on Strug's next vault?

Karolyi replied that the team definitely needed her. Not only would Strug be called upon to deliver the vault of a lifetime, she would have to do it with an injured ankle.

Putting aside the pain, Strug charged down the runway and gave it everything she had. She landed a spectacular vault! Later the team learned that her heroics had not been necessary after all because the Russians had faltered.

But Strug didn't know that at the time. She did what she needed to do when she needed to do it. She didn't ask if she could act later. She didn't wait until the circumstances were right.

Years later, Strug looks back with satisfaction at the way she was able to put the team's needs before her own.

You can ask, as Strug did, "Do we need this?" The answer is yes. Someone needs what you have to offer, and the time to offer it is now.

YOU ARE AN EXPERT!

Have you ever wanted to be an expert on something? Well, you are. If you're like most people, you are an expert on instantly changing from lazy to unlazy.

Here's the proof.

When do most people do their taxes? Right around the deadline in April, of course.

When do most college students study for their finals? At the last minute.

Writers get over writer's block in a hurry when the clock ticks toward deadline.

In all three cases, nothing changes except the clock. People don't suddenly feel like doing their taxes just because April comes. It's just that they have no choice.

Students don't suddenly become interested in their subjects just because it's the night before an exam. It's just that there's no time left.

And writers aren't any more inspired on deadline than they were earlier in the day. It's just that they have to fill the blank computer screen.

So here's a thought: As long as you have to do it anyway, why not switch from lazy to unlazy a little sooner? By doing it earlier you may wind up doing it better.

You are an expert on quickly going from lazy to unlazy. Today is the perfect day to use your expertise.

WWOT? WWOS?

Many people wait for the circumstances to be perfect before they do anything. That would be analogous to waiting for the weather to be perfect before they step outside. It just doesn't work that way.

Have you ever heard the acronym "MOOMBA?" It stands for "My Only Obstacle May Be Attitude."

In sport psychology classes, Dr. Gilbert asks the students if they know the words to *Happy Birthday*. Yes, of course they do. Then he asks if they've ever sung *Happy Birthday*. Well, of course they have. Finally, he asks someone to come to the front of the room and sing. That's when every yes turns into a no.

What is holding these students back? What is their obstacle? It's attitude, pure and simple.

They're being held back by something that can be expressed through two more acronyms.

"**WWOT?**" This stands for "What will others think?"

"**WWOS?**" This stands for "What will others say?"

You can take care of this with an acronym of your own:

"**WSIC?**" That stands for "Why should I care?"

That's right. Why should you care what others think? There's a saying that those who insist that something is impossible will always be passed up by people who are actually doing it.

Stop wondering what people will think, and start showing them what you can do!

THE WRONG WAY TO BE THE BEST

Zeke Bonura was a big-league baseball player decades ago. He was a decent hitter and he even led the league in fielding percentage twice. But he's not remembered for the balls he hit or the balls he caught. He's remembered for the balls he never touched.

The reason Bonura had such a high fielding percentage was that he seldom moved for a ball. He caught the ones that came right to him, but he just waved at the others.

No matter what field you're in, this is a perfect way to avoid making errors. Just never try too hard.

Why bother if there's a chance things might not turn out right? Why experience the pain of failure if you can possibly avoid it?

This is the wrong way to become the best. If you win while holding back, all you've learned is how to hold back.

If you go through life playing it safe, you make the biggest error of all, which is never finding out how good you could be.

Bonura's career came to an end in 1940. No longer could he go after any balls, whether hard or easy.

Your career, like Bonura's, will last only so long. Right now it doesn't feel that way. Your future is spread out so far it may seem endless. But it's not. There's only so much time for you to do things!

Don't be like Zeke Bonura. Today, go after the tough chances as well as the easy ones. You may be astonished at the balls you catch!

THE BEST TIME TO PLANT A TREE

Do you ever feel that you can't win no matter what you do? You can change that immediately. Here's a simple way to make sure you win first thing in the morning.

Just promise yourself that you will do something productive within 15 minutes of waking up. Then make sure you do it every day, without fail.

It doesn't matter exactly what this thing is. It could be something as simple as getting out of bed! In fact, the smaller the better, because if you choose something too difficult, you may get tired and stop.

Every time you do your simple action, you will feel better about yourself. You will find an increased control over your life. You'll become eager to become successful at other things.

There's a saying that the best time to plant a tree is 20 years ago. The next-best time is today.

You can't do **anything** about being lazy 20 years ago, but you can do **everything** about what you do today.

Winning is a habit, and you can start your winning habits today.

LESSON FROM A HARVARD PROFESSOR

The hardest part is getting started. The ancient Chinese philosopher Lao Tsu said, "A journey of a thousand miles must begin with a single step."

Onetime Harvard economics professor John Kenneth Galbraith learned to take that first step. He was once asked what he had learned from his years of writing. He replied, "The quality of the writing I do on days when I don't feel like writing is just as good as the quality of the writing I do on days when I do feel like writing."

Galbraith didn't wait until he felt like a writer to write. You don't have to wait until you feel like a superstar athlete to work out. You don't have to feel like a scholar to study.

Michael Jordan is one of the best basketball players in history. If you were to play against him in his prime, he would probably be taller than you. He would probably be faster, and he would have a better shot. You couldn't compete with him in those areas.

But there would be nothing to stop you from being as focused as Jordan, or from having his great attitude toward the game. Correction. There would be nothing to stop you except your own attitude.

It's just about going from lazy to unlazy.

Today you can take the first steps toward not stopping yourself.

HOW A FLOWER CHANGED EVERYTHING

One little action can set in motion a chain of success. A woman once received a flower from her boyfriend. She wanted to put the gift into a vase, but the vase was dirty. So she washed it and put the flower in.

Admiring the flower and the vase, the woman noticed that the table on which they were resting was dirty, so she cleaned it up. But a clean table looked out of place in a cluttered room, so she went to work on the whole room.

Finally, the woman looked at the house and wondered why only one room should be clean. So she cleaned the house.

We're not sure if the woman was feeling lazy when the boyfriend's flower arrived. If she was, that one flower quickly made her unlazy. It started a chain of activity that led to achievement.

If you want to become unlazy, it might be useful to find your own version of the flower. What person, place or thing will start a chain of action for you?

Here's an example. If you should be working on a report but don't feel like it, sit down at your desk. This simple action makes it more likely that you will work. Then do some more simple things. Put your feet flat on the floor. Turn off the radio. Open a book. Each of these actions will bring you closer to doing what really matters.

Find a flower in your life today!

UNLAZY HALL OF FAME
J.K. Rowling

Children all over the world have come to know Harry Potter through the storytelling of J.K. Rowling, but none of the adventures would have seen the light without the passion and persistence of the author.

Rowling had hit a low point in her life when her marriage failed and she found herself with a child and no job. Instead of giving in to sadness and despair, Rowling decided to pursue what she loved.

She took a course to gain her teaching certificate, and in her spare time she wrote. And wrote. And wrote.

When Rowling finally completed the work and found someone to represent her, she had to endure 12 rejections. On the lucky 13th try, Rowling found a publisher willing to take a chance. You know the rest, especially if you've read any of her Harry Potter books.

You can do what Rowling did. You can find something to love, and then keep doing it until success comes your way. It really is that simple.

You don't have to write books. You can play an instrument, invent a product, practice your sport, anything you love to do or must do.

There's one more thing. You have to keep trying when you come up against rejection. You have to go back once, twice, as many times as it takes! Rowling hit the jackpot on her 13th attempt. People will say that she was lucky. Her story tells us otherwise.

"The important thing is this: to be able at any moment to sacrifice that which we are for what we could become." — CHARLES Du BOS

HOW TO WIN A MARATHON

One thing you might see on the wall of a runners' store is an Adidas poster ...

"Sweat, pain, and exhaustion are all temporary — finishing Boston is forever."

This poster refers to the Boston Marathon. Even if you're not a runner, this message pertains to you because you're also in a marathon. For example, if you're in college, getting your degree is a marathon – not a sprint. Losing weight is a marathon – not a sprint. Life itself is a marathon, not a sprint.

Whether it's an athletic marathon, an academic marathon or a weight-loss marathon, there are two things you have to do to cross the finish line:

1. Start.
2. Continue.

Sounds simple ... but it's not that easy. Aesop knew that when he wrote the fable about the tortoise and the hare. You remember hearing it as a kid. A tortoise and the hare have a race. The speedy hare jumps out to a lead against the plodding tortoise.

Confident – too confident – the hare falls asleep, only to wake in time to see the tortoise nearing the finish line. Despite a burst of speed, the hare loses.

It's great if you decide to take the first step. But you must take the rest of the steps, too.

INSTANT ATTITUDE ADJUSTMENT

Why do so many people fail to continue once they get started? The No. 1 reason for marathon runners is pain and exhaustion. The No. 1 reason for the rest of us is discouragement. Whether you're a runner or not, in the long run, it hurts more to quit than to continue.

QUESTION: How do you fight discouragement?
ANSWER: With success.

Let us explain ...

Nothing succeeds like success. When you actually start seeing results, your whole world changes. **RESULTS CHANGE ATTITUDES.** When you actually start seeing weight loss or better grades, these results are powerful motivators. Nothing succeeds like success.

Graduating from college isn't easy, but if you take tests and pass them, you can use that success to get more success. When you add up all the successes, you will have a graduation cap and gown.

Let's say you're in medical school and you graduate with the lowest grade-point average in your class. What do you think others are going to call you? Dummy? Last? No. If you graduate last in your class at medical school, people will call you "Doctor."

All those successes may not have been spectacular ones. But, piled one atop the other, they were enough to get you through medical school. Let success be the fuel that powers you past discouragement.

HOW TO *REALLY* STUDY
(Dr. Gilbert speaking)

George Makdis was a biology major with a 3.93 grade-point average at Montclair State. When he spoke to one of my classes, I asked him if his academic success came from being smarter than other students. He said, "Absolutely not!" George said that any student could get the grades he did IF that student studied like he did. Basically, George was saying that he isn't smarter than other students. He just studies smarter!

As a matter of fact, George earned much higher grades at Montclair State than he ever did when he was in high school. Why??? George said that he was lazy in high school. Oh, not on the football field, where he was a star. He was lazy in the classroom. But once he decided that he wanted to be a doctor, that laziness disappeared and was replaced by focused energy.

Superstar sales trainer Frank Somma always says the same thing when he speaks to my classes: "I hire for attitude and train for skill." Somma has neither the time nor the wish to change people's attitudes.

When George changed his attitude between high school and college, his approach to study changed, too. He didn't get any smarter, he just started doing a better job with the smarts he had.

You can do what he did **WHEN YOU GET UNLAZY**.

TWO GUARANTEES

What do you have to do to get into the very best shape of your life? Whether you want to lose weight, gain muscle, stop smoking or start running, if you're going to make changes, there are two things that are guaranteed:

1. It's going to be difficult.
2. It will be worth it.

When we think about difficulty, we're reminded of one of our all-time favorite movie scenes. In "A League of Their Own," Geena Davis, the star pitcher, tells her manager, Tom Hanks, that she is quitting baseball because it is too hard. "It's supposed to be hard," Hanks replies. "If it wasn't hard, everyone would do it. *The hard is what makes it great.*"

If it were easy to get in shape, everyone would do it.

If it were easy to quit smoking, everyone would do it.

If it were easy to gain a skill, everyone would do it.

All those things are difficult. But doing those things will separate you from others.

Here's even better news: These things are difficult, but they're not *too* difficult. Millions of people have tried and succeeded. That means it is possible. Remember the difference between winners and others. Some people say, "It may be possible, but it's too difficult." Winners say, "It may be difficult, but it's possible."

Which side of the coin will you focus on: the difficulty or the possibility? Tom Hanks said it best: "The hard is what makes it great."

WELCOMING DISCOMFORT

The key with any self-improvement program is to learn **how to be comfortable with being uncomfortable.**

Whatever change you're going to make in your lifestyle, you can expect discomfort. But you will adapt. And once you learn how to be comfortable with being uncomfortable, the next thing is to *welcome* the discomfort.

For example, if you *really* want to lose weight, feeling hungry is a good sign – not a bad sign. It's a good sign because it means you are burning up more calories than you're taking in. In other words, you're doing exactly what you want to do – you are losing weight. So *welcome* the feeling of hunger!

And if you really want to get stronger, that painful feeling you get in your arms while you're lifting weights is a good sign. It's a good sign because the fatigue you feel initiates muscular growth! In other words, you're doing exactly what you want to do – you're gaining strength. So *welcome* the feeling of fatigue!

If you're working on an idea for work or for school, that mental exhaustion is a good sign because it shows that you are exercising your creative muscles.

Life often is like the sport of orienteering. Have you ever heard of it? You start in unfamiliar territory and must use a map and a compass to find your way. This sport never lets you feel comfortable, but the satisfaction after you find your way is immense.

Same way with you. No matter what you're trying to accomplish, discomfort is a sign of growth. So welcome the discomfort!

INTERVENTION
(Dr. Gilbert speaking)

Now and then, during my classroom lectures, I can feel the energy leaving the room.

My students look like they are auditioning for the movie "Coma." When they act like that, the only words that can get them excited are "class cancelled."

This is when they need an intervention, something that will quickly change their energy level.

My intervention??? A game of Simon Says.

That's right. This simple game you played as a kid is really about the game of life. Simon Says gets you from sitting to standing, from thinking to doing, from serious to fun, from low energy to high energy.

I've played Simon Says hundreds of times when talking to sports teams, business conferences and parent groups. It never fails to break the ice and put energy into the audience. Why?

Simon Says is all about movement and being involved. It makes you part of the game and lets you laugh. It's so much better than sitting in a lecture hall and being preached to. A speaker in a lecture hall *wants* you to be part of what is going on. A game of Simon Says *lets* you be part of it.

That's why it's so important to find something you love. You get involved, your energy begins to flow, and suddenly you don't feel lazy any more.

Simon Says, " Find something you love to do and do it!"

GREAT EXCUSES
(Coach Tully speaking)

A few summers ago, my daughter Katie and I were headed for an outdoor concert.

We had tickets on the lawn, while much of the crowd – and the band – would be under shelter.

That meant that the show would go on, despite the wind, rain, thunder and lightning we were experiencing.

We could barely see as we drove. We stopped once. We listened to the radio for any hope that the storm would pass.

There's just one thing we didn't do. We never said one word about turning around and going home. We wanted to see the show, and gave no thought to not seeing it. And we saw it!

Funny thing about that storm. If we had been going to school, to work or on an annoying errand, it would have been a perfect excuse not to go.

It's the same way with you. Lots of the reasons you give yourself for not doing something are just excuses.

In Juneau, Alaska, where it rains about 220 days per year, people say they never postpone an event because of bad weather. If they did, they could never get anything done. They don't use weather as an excuse.

How about you? When you decide not to do something, do you have a reason or an excuse?

THE GRASS IS GREEN IN COPLEY SQUARE
(Dr. Gilbert speaking)

Simon Says is more than a game. It's what psychologists call a pattern interruption: doing something dramatically different and totally unexpected.

Suppose you've been working at your desk on your computer all day. You're starting to feel psychologically fatigued. If you take a break and sit around having coffee with co-workers and talking about the work you've been doing – that is NOT a pattern interruption. That's doing more of the same. Instead, do something radically different.

Let me tell you when I first got introduced to the concept of pattern interruptions.

It was September 1959, the first day of school, and I was an eighth-grade student at Boston Latin School. Thirty of us walked into Room 115 for Mr. Jameson's Latin class.

Like any other teacher, Mr. Jameson began that class by taking the roll. Then, unlike any other teacher, he asked THE QUESTION: "What time is it?"

Some of us looked at our watches. Some of us looked at the clock right above the door. And some of us just looked confused.

"No, no, no," he exploded. "Whenever I ask you THE QUESTION, I want you to stand up."

We stood up not knowing what to expect.

Then, he said, "I want you to sing this song:"

The grass is green
in Copley Square,
Copley Square, Copley Square.
The grass is green
in Copley Square ...
(Then with a big, dramatic finish)
Cop-ley Square!

This went to the tune of the children's song, *This is the Way We Wash Our Clothes*.

Mr. Jameson enthusiastically conducted.

When the song was over, he waved his hands and directed us to take our seats.

As we sat down, we looked at each other with question marks on our faces. None of us knew what to make of all this.

And this wasn't just a first-day-of-class trick. It became a ritual. At least once every week or two, Mr. Jameson would ask THE QUESTION and we'd obediently stand up, sing *Copley Square,* then sit back down. This went on for the entire school year.

And when did Mr. Jameson ask us THE QUESTION? When our eyes were glazed over. When, like my students today, we looked like we could have been auditioning for the movie *Coma*.

Invent your own pattern interruptions. Go for a walk. Look at the sky. Chew some bubble gum. Take a day off and go to the zoo. And when in Boston, visit Copley Square.

When you're done, you'll be refreshed and ready to work.

LITTLE THINGS AND BIG THINGS

Have you ever been bitten by a mosquito? Probably. Have you ever been bitten by an elephant? Probably not.

Why are we asking such an obvious question? To make a point that may not be quite so obvious. It's not the big things in life that get you. It's the little things. You get more problems from inconveniences than you do from catastrophes.

Your life is about one simple task: You have to make sure that little things don't turn into big things.

For instance, is it OK to be lazy now and then? Of course. Everyone needs a mental health day now and then. It's when laziness becomes a pattern that you have a problem.

It's OK to take a nap on the couch, but when you become a couch potato, a little thing has become a big thing. Spending your life on the couch will drain all your energy and purpose. Getting off the couch can do the opposite.

Remember, when a little thing becomes a big habit, you're in big trouble.

B.Y.O.B.

You can either have a boss or be a boss.

Most people need someone to tell them when to get to work and what to do when they get there. These people will always have a boss.

But if you're the kind of person who knows what to do and then does it, you can be a boss.

It's your choice. Will you B.Y.O.B.? Be Your Own Boss?

Hall of Fame athletes Larry Bird and Jerry Rice never needed anyone to tell them what to do. They practiced harder than anyone.

They never needed anyone to tell them when to show up. They showed up before anyone.

One of the most inspiring parts of the Olympics is the Opening Ceremony. Even though there are thousands of athletes in dozens of events present, there are two common denominators.

First, all these athletes went through days when they didn't feel like doing what they needed to do. They did it anyway, and that's why they wound up in the Olympics.

Second, they all have a coach. Don't confuse having a coach with having a boss. A boss is a supervisor. A coach is a partner in achievement. World-class athletes don't need to be told what to do. They already know that. They need feedback on how well they're doing it. When you get unlazy, you can move from having a boss to having a coach.

IT'S NOT DIFFICULT

Dr. Gilbert loves to do magic tricks. He can tear up a newspaper and put it back together. He can guess a word you picked out in a 200-page book. He can tell you what day of the week you were born, astonish you with a card trick, or rip apart a belt that resisted the power of the strongest people in the audience.

He performs these tricks in class for his students, in diners for the servers and just about anyplace where he thinks he can make a point.

His point is that the tricks are not difficult; they are merely time consuming. They are the result of hours and hours of practice.

In fact, if you knew how these tricks were performed, you would be disappointed. The tricks aren't really magic; they are common sense disguised as magic.

It's the same way with your studies, your job, or your sport. If you put in the hours and hours needed to improve, you can astonish people. Open-mouthed with wonder, they will want to know your secret.

When you tell them, they will be disappointed. Your astonishing trick is nothing more than finding the right strategy and then practicing.

This formula works for playing the piano, juggling, writing, anything in your life!

Remember: It's not difficult. It's just time consuming.

BABY'S FIRST STEP

For parents, few things rival the thrill of baby's first step. The proud mom and dad eagerly await the event. They're ready with their iPhone cam. They call their friends and family to tell them the news.

No wonder! Taking that first step is a huge moment for any baby. It separates the past from the future, and opens the way to a different life.

You're just like a baby in the sense that life is full of first steps. You can go from out-of-shape to buff, from addicted to sober, from sick to healthy, or from jobless to employed. In each case, that first step is the one that can transform everything. Nothing can happen without it.

Just as with a baby, that first step isn't easy. You may fall a few times. You may be a bit wobbly on your feet. But those things are soon forgotten when you're on your way to a new life.

If you're not getting what you want from life, you can change it all with that one step. You can start doing something you haven't been doing, or you can stop doing something harmful.

Tennis legend Martina Navratilova took a big step in her life. Years ago, after winning one or two prestigious tournaments, she faced a choice: She could rest on her laurels or become one of the all-time greats. She chose greatness, and began by overhauling her diet. Navratilova became great, maybe the greatest of all time. It began with the one step of fixing her diet.

What step can you take today that will transform your life?

YOUR RESUME DOESN'T MATTER

Bill Porter is one of the most famous salesmen in history. He became a legend in door-to-door sales despite cerebral palsy. He was even immortalized in the TV film "Door to Door." Whenever he was rejected, he simply repeated his mantra, "The next person will say yes."

In other words, what was inside him was way more important than any physical characteristic. Think of it this way: **Everyone gets rejected; some people just handle it better than others.** This is true everywhere in your life. It's not what happens to you, it's how you respond to what happens to you that determines the outcome.

Let's use asparagus to make a point. Some people love asparagus. Some people hate it. The point is, it's not the asparagus. It's the way people react to it.

Everything in life is like asparagus. Adversity? It's all about the way you react to it. Obstacles? It's all in the way you react to them. Success? It's all in the way you handle it.

All these are situations in which if you just change your response, you can change your results.

The thing you call laziness – or that other people see as laziness in you – is just a response to opportunities that have arisen. These opportunities are there for you every day, and you can change your response to them any time you want.

If you don't change the way you react to opportunities, the things on your resume – no matter how impressive – can't help you when problems arise.

UNLAZY HALL OF FAME
Grete Waitz

Grete Waitz dominated the New York City Marathon as few athletes have ever dominated any event, winning it nine times in little more than a decade.

In just two sentences, she explains why she became so successful, and how you can become successful, too.

"I prefer to train in the dark, cold winter months when it takes a stern attitude to get out of bed before dawn and head out the door to below-freezing weather conditions," she said. "Anyone can run on a nice, warm, brisk day."

No wonder Waitz accomplished what she did! She had found a perfect formula. Just practice in a way that no one else is willing to, and then enjoy the rewards.

If you want things that other people want, you must be willing to do things that other people are not willing to do.

Like Grete Waitz, you can run with others when the weather is nice. Like Waitz, you can also run on days when those people do not feel like it.

Here's a strategy to help you do it. Just promise yourself that you will run every day, no matter what the conditions. Once you build your day around the idea that running is your top priority, the habit will kick in.

You can use the same strategy in any area of life, whether it's studying, playing a musical instrument, etc. Once you do that, you will rise to a level you never thought possible.

ADVERSITY CREATES HEROES

Maybe you've never thought of yourself as a hero. You are closer than you think. In fact, you are only one decision away from becoming a hero bigger than Spiderman and Wonder Woman put together.

You just have to decide what to do about your laziness. Olympic ski champ Picabo Street said, "Adversity creates heroes." Well, laziness is your adversity. It's something that can frustrate you, overwhelm you, defeat you.

It doesn't have to be that way. The minute you decide to become unlazy, there's no telling what you can accomplish.

When the comic book *Superman* first appeared, Superman didn't have any weaknesses. He could jump higher than buildings, see through walls, and fly! Before very long, that story line became old. No one could relate to a hero who didn't have problems.

Soon Superman had problems. The reading public learned he was vulnerable to kryptonite, to magic and to the schemes of villains who tried to destroy him. All of a sudden, the audience could identify with this hero.

It's the same way with you. You can't be a hero without problems and obstacles to overcome. In fact, it's by overcoming these obstacles that you become a hero.

Right now your kryptonite is laziness. It's the thing that is killing your dreams.

Decide to write a story about unlikely success, and make yourself the hero. The more laziness you must overcome, the better your story will be!

HOW TO BE THE HARDEST WORKER

There's a saying that no one works harder than a curious child.

Well, almost no one.

Albert Einstein said, "I am no genius. I am merely very curious."

Einstein wondered about the nature of the universe. "I want to know God's thoughts," he said. He wanted to know, for instance, what it would be like to ride on a beam of light. His obsession with the beam of light led him to the Theory of Relativity.

You don't have to discover relativity. That's already been done. But everyone has things they wonder about. In following your curiosity, you will begin to do things you never thought you would do. You might get up earlier, get to work earlier, stay later.

It's not because you want to want to get up earlier. It's that your curiosity will override all the obstacles.

If you become as curious as a 2-year-old or Einstein, you will no longer be lazy. You may wind up working harder than anyone – and loving it!

STEP BY STEP

Suppose it's your first day of college. You wake up and you're overwhelmed. You don't know where the classrooms are. You don't even know which building is which. You don't know what your first course is all about, and you've told everyone you're a pre-med major and you're going to be a doctor one day.

On your way around campus, you are paralyzed by fear. Fortunately, a wise old professor walks by. He's very familiar with the look you have in your eyes. He asks what's wrong.

You say, "My whole life I wanted to be a doctor, and now I realize I'm never going to get into medical school."

He says, "What's your grade-point average?"

You reply, "I don't have one. This is my first day."

The professor smiles and says, "All you have to worry about is going to your classes today and studying three hours in the library this evening. Can you do that?"

You answer, "I guess I could."

The professor then says, "If you really want to be a doctor, your 'I guess I could' will become a 'Yes, I will.'"

With that, the professor reaches into his pocket and takes out a business card. "Call me tomorrow," he says, "and I'll tell you the next thing you have to do to get into medical school."

The student says, "Thank you very much, but I really don't think you helped me."

"Trust me," the professor says. "I've given you the best advice anybody could give you."

Despite his skepticism, the student for some reason calls the professor, who gives him the same advice. "Go to class and study."

With the professor's help, the student suddenly gets it. Success is just a matter of doing things step by step. This goes for medical school, sports or business.

Whenever you're tempted to get overwhelmed, just follow the professor's advice. Just do the right thing right now.

FINDING A COACH

Fast forward 20 years. The college student did get into medical school. He's a success, and he has a wonderful family. But he's also become an alcoholic. One day a wise old physician in the hospital approaches him and inquires, "What are you doing tonight at seven?"

Before the doctor can offer an excuse, the wise old doctor says, "Meet me here." At seven the two of them go to a meeting of Alcoholics Anonymous.

The next day, the wise old doctor asks the same question, and they wind up going to another meeting.

Just as he did years ago, the young doctor finds himself going step by step. Today the steps are different than they were back in college, but in either case the steps are needed.

These stories are not really about a medical student and a wise old professor. They're about you and your coach.

"But," you protest, "I don't have a coach."

Well, that's not really true. Whether you know it or not, you are surrounded by coaches. There are people who will give you advice on your health and on your career. There are videos and college courses.

There's no question that you have a coach. The only question is whether you're going to be coachable. We believe the answer is yes because you are being coached right now. But we don't know what you do for a living or the areas in which you may need guidance. Right now, find someone who can help you take the next step.

WHO AM I TO SUCCEED?

You have no idea of the power you have. Suppose you're driving into New York City and your car breaks down in the Lincoln Tunnel. It's 8 a.m., and it will take hours for the traffic jam to clear.

Do you realize you have affected hundreds of interviews, thousands of meetings? You've been on the news in the metropolitan area. Just you and your car did all this.

You can make a huge difference in the world, either in a negative way or in a positive way. We're not religious experts, but it seems that every major religion started with one person. The Civil Rights movement was started by Rosa Parks. Baseball was integrated by one player – Jackie Robinson.

Thomas Jefferson said, "One person with courage is a majority." It takes a whole lot of courage to do things you haven't done before. Just think of the 10 most powerful words in the English language: "If it is to be, it is up to me."

If you're ever tempted to ask, "But who am I to accomplish great things?" we have an answer for you. You are just as qualified as anyone to make a big difference. The greatest antidote to laziness is to feel that you are making a difference.

Who do you think is going to be more motivated? The person who just wants to get into medical school, or the person who wants to cure cancer? Getting into school is a career goal. Curing cancer is a life mission. Find your mission today.

HURT, PAIN, AGONY

Maybe you've heard the saying, "In the world of the blind, the person with one eye is king."

Same way with you. In the world of the lazy, someone who does even a little bit is king.

We're not asking you to be unlazy 24 hours a day. Two hours a day will do it.

The greatest college swimming coach of all time was Doc Counsilman. Over his pool at Indiana University was a banner with three words: hurt, pain, agony.

The first day of practice every fall, Counsilman brought all the would-be swimmers out on the pool deck, pointed to the banner and said, "If you want to make this team you have to come here for two hours until you hurt. If you have higher goals and you want to be a national champ, you have to come here every afternoon and swim until you are in pain. If you want to be a world or Olympic champ, you have to swim until you are in agony."

Hurt, pain or agony, the choice was up to them.

Some chose hurt. Some chose pain. Some chose agony. The interesting thing is that a few minutes after practice, when all had showered and left, they were all back to normal.

They didn't have to be super ambitious for the other 22 hours. They just had to make a choice for those two hours.

You get to make a similar choice every day.

TRAFFIC SIGNALS

Let's say you wake up one morning and a strange idea hits you. "I'm not going to go to work unless all the traffic lights are green," you say.

So you get up, you get dressed and head to work. Three lights down the road, you stop because it is red. You turn around and go home.

Sound silly?

No, it's tragic because some people live their lives this way. They want all the lights to be green. They're bound to be disappointed. Everything is never going to go in their direction. There will always be red lights.

But some people don't even wait for the light to turn red. They turn around at the first sight of amber!

More students drop out of college in September than in the rest of the year combined. We know of a student who dropped out of school because he couldn't find a parking space.

There's a word for high-level unlaziness. It's called "resilience." It's what makes some people stay on the road when the light turns red. It's what makes some people stay in the game when the score is against them, and stay in business when obstacles arise.

For many years, legendary baseball slugger Babe Ruth held the record for most times striking out. He once was asked what he thought about when he struck out. He said, "I think about hitting home runs."

"In life, it's rarely about getting a chance; it's about taking a chance. You'll never be 100% sure it will work, but you can always be 100% sure doing nothing won't work." — MARKESA YEAGER

SHAKE IT OFF AND STEP UP

One day on a ranch, a baby donkey asked grandpa, "How can I grow up to be big and strong like you?"

"That's simple," said the elder donkey. "You just have to learn how to do two things: shake it off and step up."

Then the grandpa told this story: Once upon a time a donkey fell into a well. The farmers came by, saw what happened and discussed what to do. They decided that getting the donkey out of the well was not worth the trouble, and they didn't want anyone to fall in, so they began to fill the shaft with dirt.

Each time a shovelful came down, the donkey shook it off and stepped up. The farmers kept shoveling, and the donkey kept shaking, and they kept shoveling and the donkey kept stepping up. Sure enough, the farmers soon filled the well! They filled it to the brim, so the donkey was able to step right out, and never worry about falling back in!

You're going to have dirt shoveled on you every day in the form of gossip, criticism, negative comments. And this won't come only from the outside, but from the inside as well. Your biggest critic might be yourself. Your biggest de-motivator might be yourself.

No matter where the dirt comes from, you've got to be as smart as a donkey. Instead of letting the dirt bury you, just shake it off and step up.

There's no guarantee that the critics will ever stop shoveling, but if you keep shaking it off and stepping up, it won't matter.

UNLAZY HALL OF FAME
Doc Counsilman

It's one thing to be a legend and another thing to add to your legend.

That's what happened in the case of swimming coach Doc Counsilman, who won titles at Indiana University and coached the U.S. swim team in the 1964 and 1976 Olympics.

Those feats were nothing compared to what he accomplished when he was in his fifties.

Four years after being diagnosed with Parkinson's Disease, Counsilman set his mind toward swimming the English Channel, one of the most challenging feats that a human can attempt.

In 1979, Counsilman completed his quest, becoming the oldest person at that time to make the crossing.

If he can do something like that, you can, too! You are just one choice away from greatness:

Imagine if you start walking a mile a day.

Imagine if you start taking in 200 fewer calories a day.

Imagine if you practice the violin every day.

It may be hard to get going today, but that pain is nothing compared to the regret you would feel if you never get started.

THE 80-20 RULE

Have you ever heard of the 80-20 rule? Developed by management consultant Joseph M. Juran, it says that about 80 percent of the effects come from 20 percent of the causes. For example, 80 percent of the sales are made by 20 percent of the salesmen.

This principle can help you become unlazy. When you hang around ambitious people, you might get infected with the ambition bug. There's a saying, "If you want to run fast, run alone. If you want to run far, run with others."

If you want to get unlazy about studying, find someone who studies a lot. If you want to get unlazy about working out, go to a health club. There you will find yourself surrounded by people who work out a lot.

We have no way of knowing whether these people actually feel like studying or working out. It doesn't matter whether they feel like it.

What really matters is that they do it.

There is a tennis club outside Moscow that is renowned for producing world-class players. In fact, at one point, five of the top 10 female players in the world had been trained by the same coach there.

When these players went to the club, they were always surrounded by people who cared about tennis excellence. It's hard to be around those people without picking up some of their passion.

So use the 80-20 principle. Hang around with the 20 percent of people who produce 80 percent of the results.

BUILDING ROME

A little girl says to her mom, "How long does this popcorn have to be in the microwave?"

"Seven minutes," replies the mother.

"That's too long," the girl says.

This conversation happens all the time in some form. People want things right away, and if that doesn't happen, they give up.

The world is more immediate than ever. When you were a kid, you listened to your favorite radio station on a transistor radio and had to wait to hear your favorite song. Now you can program that same song into your iPod and hear it any time you want.

You no longer have to walk into the bank; you can go through the drive-in. You don't have to go to the library because you can do your research on your iPhone.

This instant gratification is the enemy of quality. Good things take time. You can't graduate in one semester. You can't learn to play the guitar in one lesson. Rome wasn't built in a day, and if you want proof, go to Rome and see cathedrals that took centuries to build.

If you want to be a little better than you are now, get a little bit unlazy. If you want to be better than some of your opponents, be unlazy more than now and then. If you want to be better than most, find a way to be unlazy every day.

ENTERTAINMENT VS. FULFILLMENT

Many people watch TV as if they were paid to do it. They put in dozens of hours every week. Trouble is that they don't get paid for it. In fact, they rarely get any return at all.

As proof, ask yourself this question: Have you ever felt fulfilled watching TV? Probably not. You've been entertained, but not fulfilled. Most people settle for that. They would rather be entertained than fulfilled. They would rather be watching the marathon than running in it.

They have not yet discovered the secret: Feeling good about something you accomplished is better than the best show on television. It's a feeling that lasts longer, and it leads to more good feelings.

Entertainment is about being a spectator. It's about being on the sidelines. Fulfillment comes from being involved, from being in the middle of things.

There's no harm in relaxing with some entertainment now and then, but when the television set puts you on the couch, on the outside looking in, then it's a problem. It means you've gotten lazy.

This doesn't mean you have to start running a marathon. That might not be good for you. Here's what would be good for you: Think of something that will leave you with a feeling of satisfaction, then do it. Maybe it's cleaning a room or running an overdue errand.

No matter how small that something is, it will feel better than sitting in front of the TV all night long.

CHAPTER SEVEN

THE NEW YOU

"I'm not funny. What I am is brave."
— LUCILLE BALL

"You will never find time for anything. If you want time you must make it."
— CHARLES BUXTON

"Fear not that life shall come to an end, but rather fear that it shall never have a beginning."
— JOHN HENRY CARDINAL NEWMAN

"If you would one day renovate yourself, do so from day to day. Yea, let there be daily renovation."
— CONFUCIAN ANALECTS

"Our only security is our ability to change."
— JOHN LILLY

YOUR GAME IS JUST BEGINNING

Some people act lazy because they think the game is over:

When they lose, they think it's over.

When they're rejected, they think it's over.

When projects fall apart, they think it's over.

But it's not. No matter where you are in life, the game has just begun. That's how winners think.

Dr. Gilbert once had the chance to interview swimming champion Amanda Beard.

He asked her what her favorite motivational story was. She said she didn't have one.

He asked her what her favorite motivational quote was. She said she couldn't think of one.

Just when he thought that the interview was a waste of time, Dr. Gilbert said, "So what exactly does motivate you?"

Her answer came down to two words: "Bad swims."

Beard got motivated when she did not swim well.

That's how Beard is different from others. When some people do poorly, they go into a **slide**. When Beard does poorly, she goes on a **streak**.

You can do the same. When you lose, get excited. The game has just begun.

HOW TO DATE A SUPERMODEL

How would you like to date the person of your dreams? It's not as hard as you think. In fact, here's the way to get going: Just ask her (or him)!

If you don't ask, the answer is always no.

Dr. Gilbert learned this one day while spending some time with a bonafide international supermodel. He asked her whether she had a boyfriend. She said no. He asked her if she goes out on many dates. She said no. When he expressed surprise, she said, "No one ever asks."

Think of that. "No one ever asks."

People are so afraid of being rejected that they don't even try. Don't be one of those people.

You miss 100 percent of the shots you don't take. If you don't go to the audition, you won't get the part. If you don't try out for the team, you won't make it. If you don't make your calls, you'll never find your buyers.

The best salespeople in the world know that the best way to get a lot of sales is to get a lot of rejections. Every rejection brings you closer to a success. That means the skill isn't in getting people to say yes, but in getting past your feelings when people say no.

People start to seem lazy when in fact they're afraid of all those rejections. They stop asking. For them, the answer will always be no.

Never stop asking. The next answer might be yes!

MAYBE THEY'RE RIGHT

If you're like many people, you find it hard to accept a compliment.

When others say nice things, you don't know how to react. You might say, "I don't think so" or "I wish." You might even wind up irritating the person who was trying to be nice to you.

The next time someone says something nice to you, here's what to say: "Thank you." Why? Because maybe that someone is right. Maybe you really do have the qualities that the person says you do.

Even if you're not sure, what is the harm in believing it? Let yourself enjoy the feeling that someone admires what you do. There are plenty of critics out there. Who says that they know more than your supporters do?

Life isn't long enough for you to discover all things by yourself. Let other people do some discovering for you. They might see your sense of humor, your kindness or your calm in the face of adversity.

They might point you toward an area where you can really shine. They might see in you a writer, an artist, an athlete, a student or a leader.

Remember, when people say something nice about you, just accept the compliment and say, "Thank you." After all, maybe they're right!

LAZINESS WILL KILL YOU

Research shows there is a link between childhood obesity and having a TV in the bedroom. Kids don't even have to leave their room anymore. They can watch their favorite shows while in bed. They can munch on chips as they sit with eyes glued to whatever screen they're viewing.

No wonder stats on childhood obesity are getting more alarming each day! Yes, sugar, salt and fat are culprits. But so are ease, comfort and laziness. Any one of these factors can really hold you back or set you back. Together they can put you in the hospital – or worse.

Remember at the start of this book, we told you that laziness is a disease that can affect your work, your school and even your health. Thank goodness this disease can be treated instantly.

Doctors say that no matter how long you smoke cigarettes, your body begins to heal the moment you stop. The sooner you stop, the quicker the healing begins. The longer you stay stopped, the more your body heals.

It's the same way with your laziness. If you stop being lazy and start being unlazy, things get better in your life right away. If you start being unlazy and you stay unlazy, they get much better.

There's the story of a waiter who wasn't getting many tips. One day he realized that there was nothing preventing him from giving world-class service. He decided that from that moment on, he would provide the best possible experience for every diner. Suddenly, his tips went up. You can make a similar change right now!

YOUR CHOICE

In 1998, the Indianapolis Colts held the first pick in the NFL draft, and they were torn between two quarterbacks who seemed to have equally bright futures.

The Colts wound up taking Peyton Manning over Ryan Leaf, and history has justified their choice. Manning became one of the greatest players in league history, while Leaf's career has been a series of disappointments.

What happened? It came down to decisions – not the one the Colts made, but the ones the players made. Manning always delivered more than expected, and Leaf less.

It will be the same way in your life. You can wind up like Manning; you can rank with Leaf as a disappointment; you can land somewhere in between.

Let's say that again. Whatever path you follow in life – business, school, sports, the arts – you will wind up doing better than expected, worse than expected, or just about the same as expected.

It's really up to you.

Your line of work may not get as much attention as Manning's, but those around you will know whether you overachieved, underachieved or something in between.

More important, you will know. As we said way back in the beginning of this book, the feeling of underachievement can gnaw at you. Now you have the tools to achieve.

THE CONVERSATION THAT NEVER HAPPENS
(Dr. Gilbert speaking)

I have spent my whole career teaching at Montclair State. One benefit of this is that your old students know where to find you. I have never had this conversation with a former student. ...

"You know, Dr. Gilbert," says the student, "I made a big mistake when I was here. I should have partied more. I should have gotten drunk more often."

That conversation has never happened.

This conversation has happened a few times:

"You know, Dr. Gilbert, if I had worked a little harder, I could have been an All-American in lacrosse." Or, "If I had studied a little more I would have gotten into medical school."

Here's a prescription for those who want to get into medical school. Put yourself in the future for a moment. Imagine that it is 20 years from now, and you have just run into one of your college professors.

What will the conversation be like? Will you be able to thank your professor for helping you on your way? Or will you have to admit that for one reason or another, you never made your dream come true?

Someone once said, "Make your decisions based not on the person that you are, but on the person you want to become."

If you want to be a doctor tomorrow, study like a doctor today.

"Don't be afraid if things seem difficult in the beginning. That's only the initial impression. The important thing is not to retreat; you have to master yourself." — OLGA KORBUT

FRUSTRATION VS. FASCINATION

Baseball player Yogi Berra famously said, "When you get to the fork in the road, take it."

All of us take that advice every day, without even realizing it. We come to the failure fork, that certain place where things aren't going the way we wish.

At the failure fork, some people react with fascination, and others with frustration. Fascination works. Frustration doesn't. Too often we choose frustration. Famous achievers never do.

Take Tom Monaghan, who founded Domino's Pizza. He faced one difficulty after another in trying to establish his business. He always responded by trying to solve problems instead of running from them.

George Westinghouse solved a problem that made trains safer. Until he came along, when the brake system failed, trains wouldn't stop. Westinghouse, thinking outside the box, invented brakes in which if the system failed, the brakes would automatically be applied.

If you're a professional athlete, you can become frustrated or fascinated by strong opponents. Same way if you're in business or in school.

The quality of your life and your level of achievement will depend on whether you treat problems with frustration or fascination.

Remember, one of them works. The other one doesn't. Which one will you chose?

IT'S RIGHT THERE IN FRONT OF YOU

Years ago, Jim Murray, the late, great sports columnist for the Los Angeles Times, faced a severe case of writer's block.

With deadline approaching, he just couldn't find anything to fill the next day's column.

Finally, Murray decided that he would just look out the window and write about whatever he saw. His home happened to overlook the Pacific Ocean. When he gazed out there, he saw whales swimming past.

On most days, Murray never would have written a column about whales for an audience that was more used to reading about baseball and football.

In this case, Murray had no other ideas, so he went ahead. His audience loved it! The whale column proved to be one of his best.

Your life is a lot like Jim Murray's. There are times when you just don't know what to do. You're out of ideas. On days like that, just look around with new eyes. There might be something there that you've seen a thousand times, and now you'll notice it with appreciation.

It could be an opportunity or an insight into one of your gifts. Either way, when you look around yourself with fresh eyes, you may find something special, just like Jim Murray did.

BRUCE SPRINGSTEEN'S SECRET

Bruce Springsteen gives an insight into his life in the documentary, "The Promise: The Making of 'Darkness on the Edge of Town.'"

He says, "I didn't want to be happy. I didn't want to be famous. I didn't want to be rich. I wanted to be great."

Springsteen is describing a choice that you have. You can choose to be great.

It's like the difference between playing the air guitar and the real guitar. The air guitar players pick up a guitar, find it too difficult, then put it down. The real guitar players pick up a guitar, find it interesting, and keep trying.

Springsteen chose to learn the real guitar. It took a lot more time and sweat than playing the air guitar, but it also carried greater rewards.

By choosing to pursue what was difficult, Springsteen did achieve greatness. Along the way, he became rich and famous.

Put down your air guitar and pick up a real one. Make the choice to do what is difficult. Greatness resides on the other side of that difficulty.

Just ask Bruce Springsteen.

FLYING PENGUINS

Once upon a time, some penguins decided that they wanted to fly. They got tired of standing on the ground while other creatures flew gracefully through the air.

Acting on their thought, the penguins enrolled in a one-day flying course. In the morning, things went slowly, as the penguins tried to get the hang of things.

After lunch, things really changed. The penguins gained more confidence and began to spend more and more time in the air. Deep into the day, their confidence turned into sheer joy as the new flyers did loops and other tricks.

At 5 p.m., they flew up to the podium to get their diplomas. Finally it was time to leave. The penguins said thank you, goodbye, and then ... walked home.

They didn't use the information they had received. They went right back to familiar habits and thoughts.

You've just received your diploma in unlaziness. You know strategies for becoming unlazy, and you've seen stories of some of the all-time greats.

The question is what you're going to do with this information. You can fly home or you can walk.

We hope you do loops.

DENNIS ROGERS

What happens when you run into difficulty? Dennis Rogers gets excited. He's an internationally known strongman who can rip phone books and lift refrigerators with one hand.

Rogers wasn't born a strongman. He was a weakling who was bullied and placed into special education gym class. But he had an extraordinary reaction to those circumstances. He got energized, not discouraged.

You can see it when he performs. The greater the difficulty, the more excited Rogers becomes. That's how he became a performer who astonishes audiences all over the world.

You'd want Rogers on your team, because you surely wouldn't want him on the other team. Imagine trying to compete with someone who got more excited as the situation got more difficult?

To Rogers, there are no problems. There are only possibilities.

For him, there are no obstacles, only opportunities.

We can hear your objections right now. "I'm just not like that," you say. Not yet.

Starting right now, you can pause and choose your response to adversity. Instead of retreating, just remind yourself that you have complete control over how you respond.

It will take practice, but then again, it took Dennis Rogers lots of practice to become a world-class strongman.

THE ULTIMATE INTERVIEW ANSWER

Let's say you've just interviewed for a job you really want. You've survived the first session and have been called back for a second one.

To your amazement, the meeting consists of only one question:

"You're one of three finalists for this job. Why should we hire you and not the others?"

This is where you look the interviewer in the eye and say, "Everyone has days when they don't feel like working. I will work just as hard on the days when I don't feel like working as I will on the days when I do feel like working. No one will ever outwork me."

If you can say that and mean it, the world is yours.

You've learned the instant cure for laziness. You don't have to feel like doing something in order to do it.

Now you've removed the thing that was holding you back.

You have become unstoppable.

Welcome to the new you!

EPILOGUE

LASTING ADVICE

Every year on his birthday, Mr. D'Amato would go to his doctor for a check-up.

After conducting the exam, the doctor said, "Mr. D'Amato, you're in great shape. How old are you?"

"Well, Doc, I'm 100 today."

"You're 100?" exclaimed the doctor. "I'm not even half your age and you're in better shape than I am. How do you do it?"

"I walk five miles every day."

"Five miles? Every day? What do you do when it rains?"

Answered Mr. D'Amato, "I put on a raincoat."

ONE LAST QUOTE

"On the day of victory, no one is tired." – Arabic proverb

ONE LAST QUESTION FROM THE AUTHORS

In this book, we have given you our very best information.

QUESTION: Will these techniques work for you?
ANSWER: Yes! IF you work them.

APPENDIX

INSTANT INSPIRATION

"Trying times are not the times to stop trying." – RAY OWEN

"Two Wrights don't make a wrong, but they did make a pretty good airplane."
— UNKNOWN

"The moment you commit and quit holding back, all sorts of unforeseen incidents, meetings and material assistance will rise up to help you." — NAPOLEON HILL

"Lost time is never found again."
— THELONIUS MONK

"I long to accomplish a great and noble task, but it is my chief duty to accomplish small tasks as if they were great and noble."
— HELEN KELLER

"If at first you DO succeed, try something harder." – **ANN LANDERS, Advice columnist**

"Let me tell you the secret that has led me to my goal. My strength lies solely in my tenacity." – **LOUIS PASTEUR, Scientist**

"Perhaps the most valuable result of all education is the ability to make yourself do the thing you have to do when it ought to be done, whether you like it or not." – **THOMAS HUXLEY, Biologist**

"Winning the prize wasn't half as exciting as doing the work itself." – **MARIA GOEPPERT MAYER, Nobel prize winner in physics**

"The beginning is the most important part of the work."
– **PLATO, Greek philosopher**

"Walk your dog every day, whether you have a dog or not."
– **PAUL DUDLEY WHITE, Cardiologist**

"When it was fashionable to say, 'May the force be with you,' I said, 'The force is within you. Force yourself.'"
– **HARRISON FORD, Actor**

"Behold the turtle: He makes progress only when he sticks his neck out." – **JAMES BRYANT CONANT, Chemist**

"Generally speaking, the great achieve their greatness by industry rather than brilliance." – **BRUCE BARTON, Ad executive**

"'I can't do it' never yet accomplished anything."
– **GEORGE P. BURNHAM, Writer**

"Many people have seen their careers crash because they preferred the familiar but deadly old ways to the risky but rewarding new ways." – **NIDO R. QUBEIN, Author**

"Common sense often isn't common practice." – **DR. JENNIFER JAMES, Cultural anthropologist**

"There is only one success: to be able to spend your life in your own way." – **CHRISTOPHER MORLEY, Writer**

"Life shrinks or expands in proportion to one's courage." – **ANAIS NIN, Writer**

"In life there are no overachievers, only underestimators." – **RICH RUFFALO, Motivational speaker**

"If the failures of the world could realize how desperate half the present-day geniuses once felt, they would take heart and try again." – **FAY COMPTON, Actress**

"Problems become opportunities when the right people come together." – **ROBERT REDFORD, Actor**

"The reason why worry kills more people than work is that more people worry than work." – **ROBERT FROST, Poet**

"You're never too old to become younger." – **MAE WEST, Actress**

"My life is one long obstacle course, with me being the chief obstacle." – **JACK PAAR, TV personality**

"The horizon is not where the sky comes down. We set our own boundaries. We have the making of our own horizons. We do not have to live in walled-in spaces." – **GROVE PATTERSON, Newspaper editor**

"I'm always amazed that people will actually choose to sit in front of the television and just be savaged by stuff that belittles their intelligence." – **ALICE WALKER, Author**

"The most beautiful experience we can have is the mysterious. It is the fundamental emotion which stands at the cradle of true art and true science." – **ALBERT EINSTEIN, Physicist**

"Sometimes the best helping hand you can give is a good, firm push." – **JOANN THOMAS**

"I went for years not finishing anything. Because, of course, when you finish something you can be judged. I had poems which were rewritten so many times I suspect it was just a way of avoiding sending them out." – **ERICA JONG, Writer**

"Before today, I thought the music was in the violin. Today I learned that the music is in me." – **NICCOLO PAGANINI, Musician**

"There are two ways to reach the top of an oak tree: Climb it or sit on an acorn and wait." – **UNKNOWN**

"If you go by other people's opinions or predictions, you'll just end up talking yourself out of something. If you're running down the track of life thinking that it's impossible to break life's records, those thoughts have a funny way of sinking into your feet." – **CARL LEWIS, Olympic track champion**

"The Wright brothers flew right through the smokescreen of impossibility." – **CHARLES F. KETTERING, Inventor**

"Challenges make you discover things about yourself that you never really knew." – **CICELY TYSON, Actress**

"It is the feeling of exerting effort that exhilarates us, as a grasshopper is exhilarated by jumping. A hard job, full of impediments, is thus more satisfying than an easy job." – **H.L. MENCKEN, Journalist**

"It takes an uncommon amount of guts to put your dreams on the line, to hold them up and say, 'How good or bad am I?' That's where courage comes in." – **ERMA BOMBECK, Columnist**

"Discovery consists of looking at the same thing as everyone else and thinking something different." – **ALBERT SZENT-GYORGYI, Biochemist**

"Be brave enough to live creatively. The creative is the place where no one else has ever been. You have to leave the city of your comfort and go into the wilderness of your intuition." – **ALAN ALDA, Actor**

"The difference between the impossible and the possible lies in a person's determination." – **TOMMY LASORDA, Baseball manager**

"Some people think of discipline as a chore. For me, it's a kind of order that sets me free to fly." – **JULIE ANDREWS, British actress**

"Think of many things. Do one." – **PORTUGUESE PROVERB**

"Manufacture enthusiasm as you go and grow." – **MAGGIE KUHN, Founder, The Gray Panthers**

"Only those who dare to fail greatly can ever achieve greatly." – **ROBERT F. KENNEDY, U.S. senator**

"When you do something, do it with your might. Put your whole soul into it. Stamp it with your own personality. Be active, be energetic, be enthusiastic and faithful, and you will accomplish your object." – **RALPH WALDO EMERSON, Philosopher, poet**

"My philosophy is that not only are you responsible for your life, but doing the best at this moment puts you in the best place for the next moment." – **OPRAH WINFREY, TV personality**

"Take a risk a day – one small or bold stroke that will make you feel great once you have done it." – **SUSAN JEFFERS, Author**

"Great souls have wills; feeble ones have only wishes." – **CHINESE PROVERB**

"If you add a little to a little and do this often, soon that little will become great." – **HESIOD, Greek poet**

"There are no hopeless situations, only people who are hopeless about them." – **DINAH SHORE, Entertainer**

"Do not bother just to be better than your contemporaries or predecessors. Try to be better than yourself." – **WILLIAM FAULKNER, Writer**

"When you're sick of being sick, you'll cease being sick." – **LAO TZU, Philosopher**

"The essential thing in life is not conquering but fighting well." – **BARON PIERRE de COUBERTIN, Father of the modern Olympic games**

"The purpose of life is a life of purpose." – **ROBERT BYRNE, Author**

"It is our choices that show us what we truly are, far more than our abilities." – **J.K. ROWLING, Author**

"Don't count the days, make the days count."
– **ED AGRESTA, Motivational speaker**

"The golden opportunity you are seeking is in yourself. It is not in your environment; it is not in luck or in chance or the help of others, it is in yourself alone." – **ORISON SWETT MARDEN, Founder, Success Magazine**

"Laziness is the secret ingredient that goes into failure."
– **ROBERT HALF, Business pioneer**

"Laziness is nothing more than the habit of resting before you get tired." – **JULES RENARD, Author**

"One thing I never want to be accused of is not working."
– **DON SHULA, Football coach**

"If you wait, all that happens is that you get older."
– **MARIO ANDRETTI, Auto racer**

"When running up a hill, it is all right to give up as many times as you wish as long as your feet keep moving."
– **SHOMA MORITA, Psychiatrist**

"Success is going from failure to failure without loss of enthusiasm." – **WINSTON CHURCHILL, Statesman**

"You either have to be first, best or different."
– **LORETTA LYNN, Country singer**

"Only those who will risk going too far can possibly find out how far one can go." – **T.S. ELIOT, Writer**

"Never confuse movement with action."
– **ERNEST HEMINGWAY, Writer**

"Gardens are not made by sitting in the shade."
– **RUDYARD KIPLING, Poet**

"Most obstacles melt away when we make up our minds to walk boldly through them." – **ORISON SWETT MARDEN, Founder, Success magazine**

"You may get skinned knees and elbows, but it is worth it if you score a spectacular goal." – **MIA HAMM, Soccer star**

"We hope this book is more than just thought-provoking. We want it to be change-provoking!" – **DR. ROB GILBERT and COACH MIKE TULLY**

"How soon 'Not now' becomes 'never.'" – **MARTIN LUTHER, Religious leader**

"So much attention is paid to the aggressive sins, such as violence and cruelty and greed with all their tragic effects, that too little attention is paid to the passive sins, such as apathy and laziness, which in the long run can have a more devastating effect." – **ELEANOR ROOSEVELT, First Lady**

"Follow your bliss and the universe will open doors for you where there were only walls." – **JOSEPH CAMPBELL, Author**

"I don't wait for moods. You accomplish nothing if you do that." – **PEARL S. BUCK, Author**

"Nobody cares if you can't dance well. Just get up and dance." – **MARTHA GRAHAM, Choreographer**

IF YOU LIKED THIS BOOK ...

.. you will love the seminar! To get our CD, "Thank God You're Lazy: The Instant Cure for What's Holding You Back," email coachtully@totalgameplan.com.

Dr. Gilbert's free Success Hotline is available 24/7/365 at (973) 743-4690. Dr. Gilbert tweets the best quotes from Success Hotline at @SuccessHotline. To contact Dr. Gilbert for personal coaching, or to speak to your group, call (973) 743-4428.

Coach Tully blogs at TotalGamePlan.com and tweets at @TotalGamePlan. He's author of "The Improvement Factor: How Winners Turn Practice into Success," and co-author of "Ten Things Great Coaches Know." To contact him for a speaking engagement, call (973) 800-5836.